Für / For:

Lydia
Maria
Hildegard
Mechthilde

IMPRESSUM / IMPRINT

Copyright © 2014 Claudia Wiker
All rights reserved.

ISBN-13: 978-0615960036 (Pauls Press)
ISBN-10: 0615960030

Published by Pauls Press, Claudia Wiker, Schaumburg, Il 60173 (USA).

Art & Design by Claudia Wiker

Front Cover Design by Emil Ivanovski, VisualEtiquette, www.emilivanovski.com

Food Photography, Copyright © 2014 by Claudia Wiker:
Claudia Wiker, www.claudia-cooking.com
Stephanie Daniel (2012), www.sddesigns.me
Chen Cheng (2009), www.wisewindows.com

The following chapter photos are from www.piqs.de (2011), "Some rights reserved":
nimmersat, "Salat"; Heinz Hasselberg, Steinfurt, "280. Finger weg!"
The following photos in basic recipes are from www. iStockphoto.com (2011):
"Fresh plums close-up" ©iStockphoto.com/malhrovitz;
"Apple sauce with rolled wafer" ©iStockphoto.com/paulbinet;
"Cooking sour cherry jam" ©iStockphoto.com/lvinst;
"Elder" ©iStockphoto.com/LianeM

www.claudia-cooking.com

GERMAN DELIGHTS

Claudia Wiker

Einführung

Deutsche Lebenslust spiegelt sich im Essen wider. Die Freude auf einen schönen Braten mit Spätzle und Soße oder auf Schupfnudeln mit Sauerkraut ist immens groß, wenn Sie sich - wie ich - im Ausland für längere Zeit aufhalten. Jetzt bin ich schon mehr als sieben Jahre von zu Hause weg: Zuerst China dann USA. Doch in all diesen Jahren sind mir Deutschland, meine Familie und die süddeutschen Küche immer ganz nah gewesen. Da ich leidenschaftlich gerne koche und backe, haben mir die Rezepte meiner Großmütter, Mutter und Schwiegermutter mein Leben in der Ferne erleichtert. Die selbst gemachten Gerichte geben mir immer das schöne Gefühl von Wärme, Gemütlichkeit ein Stück von zu Hause und deutscher Lebensfreude. Neben dem heimischen Geschmackserlebnis tragen meine Rezepte auch zur ausgewogenen und gesunden Ernährung bei. Häufig werden nur natürliche Grundnahrungsmittel verwendet wie zum Beispiel: Eier, Mehl, Hefe, Butter, Zucker und Milch, Fleisch oder frisches Gemüse und Früchte aus dem Garten. Diese Zutaten sind günstig und es gibt sie so gut wie überall auf der Welt.
Viele meiner Freunde sind in den Genuss meiner Kochkünste gekommen und wollten meine Rezepte zum Nachkochen haben. Da die meisten nur Englisch verstehen, habe ich das Buch in deutscher und englischer Sprache erstellt. Natürlich auch in der Hoffnung, dass sie neben dem Kochen und Backen ein bisschen die deutsche Sprache lernen:-)
Ich wünsche allen viel Freude mit diesem Buch und "Guten Appetit"!

Introduction

The German Zest for Life is reflected by its food. The desire for a nice roast meat with spaetzle noodles and gravy or schupfnudeln (finger-shaped potato dumplings) with sauerkraut can be absolutely huge, when you live abroad for a longer while - as I do. It has been more than seven years when I left home. First I went to China and then to the USA. But during all this time, Germany, my family and the southern german cooking stayed very close. My passion for cooking and baking and the recipes of my grandmothers, my mother and mother-in-law make my life easier in the distance. The homemade dishes give me the feeling of warmness, comfort, a part from home and the german enjoyment of life. And, besides the familiar taste, the recipes helps me to keep a healthy and balanced diet. Many of my recipes are made of unprocessed basic foods like eggs, flour, yeast, butter, sugar, milk or fresh meat and fruits or vegetables from the garden. The ingredients are low in price and available nearly all over the world.
Many of my friends experienced my food and loved it so much, that they wanted the recipes for cooking by themselves. As most of them only speak english, I decided to create a cooking book in english as well as in german. With this I hoped, that they will acquire some german language skills while having a nice time with cooking or baking.
I wish everybody lots of fun with this book and "Guten Appetit"-Enjoy your meal!

Claudia Wiker

Grund-
rezepte
S. 10

Suppen
& Salate
S. 38

Nudeln &
Kartoffel-
gerichte
S. 60

Fleisch &
Geflügel
S. 74

Content

Inhalt

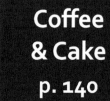

Umrechnungstabellen

Flüssigkeiten / Liquids

1000 ml	= 1 L	= approx. 34 fl oz.	= 4 cups
750 ml	= 3/4 L	= approx. 25.5 fl oz.	= 3 cups
600 ml		= approx. 20 fl oz.	= 2 1/2 cups
500 ml	= 1/2 L	= approx. 17 fl oz.	= 2 cups
375 ml	= 3/8 L	= approx. 13 fl oz.	= 1 1/2 cups
250 ml	= 1/4 L	= approx. 8 fl oz.	= 1 cup
150 ml		= approx. 5 fl oz.	= 2/3 cup
125 ml	= 1/8 L	= approx. 4 fl oz.	= 1/2 cup
100 ml	= 1 dl	= approx. 3.5 fl oz.	= 1/3 cup
50 ml		= approx. 2 fl oz.	= 1/4 cup
15 ml	= 1 EL	= approx. 0.5 fl oz.	
10 ml	= 1 cl	= approx. 0.4 fl oz.	
5 ml		= approx. 0.2 fl oz.	

Löffelmaß / Spoon

Pinch / Messerspitze	(MP)	> 0.5ml
1/8 teaspoon	Prise	0.6ml
1/4 teaspoon	1/4 Teelöffel	1.25ml
1/2 teaspoon	1/2 Teelöffel	2.5ml
1 teaspoon (tsp)	Teelöffel TL	5ml
1 tablespoon (tbsp)	Esslöffel EL	15ml

Feste Bestandteile / Dry Ingredients

1/2 oz.	= approx. 15g
1 oz.	= approx. 25g
2 oz.	= approx. 50g
3 oz.	= approx. 75g
4 oz.	= approx. 100g
6 oz.	= approx. 150g
8 oz.	= approx. 200g
9 oz.	= approx. 250g
10 oz.	= approx. 275g
11 oz.	= approx. 300g
12 oz.	= approx. 325g
13 oz.	= approx. 350g
14 oz.	= approx. 400g
15 oz.	= approx. 425g
16 oz.	= approx. 450g
17 oz.	= approx. 475g
18 oz.	= approx. 500g
19 oz.	= approx. 525g
20 oz.	= approx. 550g
26 oz.	= approx. 750g
35 oz.	= approx. 1 kg
53 oz.	= approx. 1.5 kg

Zur einfacheren Planung sind in den Rezepten folgende Angaben enthalten:

1. Schwierigkeit der Zubereitung: 1= einfache Zubereitung; 2= erfordert etwas Übung; 3= herausfordernd, erfordert viel Übung
2. Zubereitungsmenge: Angabe nach Personen
3. Zubereitungszeiten: aktive Zubereitungszeit und inaktive Zubereitungszeit (wie z.B. Koch- und Backzeiten, Kühlzeiten, Wartezeiten, etc.)

To help you plan your meals, each recipe includes the following information:

1. Grade of difficulty in preparation: 1= easy; 2= needs practice; 3= challanging
2. Amount of Servings
3. Preparation Times: active preparation times and inactive preparation times (such as cooking or baking times, cooling times, waiting times, etc.)

Conversion Tables

Mengenangaben verschiedener Lebensmittel
Food Equivalent Measurements

Zutat:	Ingredient:	1 EL / tbsp	1 TL / tsp
Backpulver	Baking Powder	10 g	3 g
Butter	Butter	10 g	4 g
Gelatine	Gelatin	10 g	3 g
Grieß	Semolina	12 g	3 g
Haferflocken	Rolled Oats	8 g	2 g
Haselnüsse (gem.)	Hazelnuts, ground	7 g	2 g
Honig	Honey	20 g	6 g
Joghurt	Yogurt	17 g	6 g
Käse, gerieben	Cheese, grated	8 g	3 g
Pulverkaffee	Coffee Powder	6 g	2 g
Kakaopulver	Cacao Powder	6 g	2 g
Kondensmilch	Condesed Milk	18 g	6 g
Mandeln (gem.)	Almonds, ground	8 g	3 g
Margarine	Margarine	10 g	4 g
Mehl	Flour	10 g	3 g
Nüsse (gem.)	Nuts, ground	8 g	3 g
Speiseöl	Cooking Oil	12 g	4 g
Paprikapulver	Paprika Powder	8 g	2 g
Puderzucker	Powder Sugar	10 g	3 g
Salatmayonnaise	Mayonnaise	15 g	5 g
Salz	Salt	15 g	5 g
Saure Sahne	Sour Cream	17 g	6 g
Süße Sahne	Cream	15 g	5 g
Semmelbrösel	Bread Crumbs	10 g	3 g
Senf	Mustard	9 g	3 g
Speisestärke	Cornstarch	9 g	3 g
Tomatenmark	Tomato Paste	19 g	5 g
Vanillezucker	Vanilla Sugar	8 g	4 g
Zimtpulver	Cinnamon Powder	6 g	2 g
Zucker	Sugar	15 g	5 g
Flüssigkeit	Liquid	15 ml	5 ml

Gasherd & Backofen
Gas Stove & Baking Oven

	Gasherd Temp. / Stove Top Temp.	F	C
Very Cool	Mark 1/3	225	105
	Mark 1/2	250	120
Cool	Mark 1	275	130
	Mark 2	300	150
Warm	Mark 3	325	165
Moderate	Mark 4	350	180
	Mark 5	375	190
Moderately Hot	Mark 6	400	200
Hot	Mark 7	425	220
	Mark 8	450	230
Very Hot	Mark 9	475	245
		500	260

Küchentechnik / Kitchen Technique

1/8" (in.)	= 0.33 cm
3/16"	= 0.47 cm
1/4"	= 0.63 cm
3/8"	= 0.95 cm
3/4"	= 1.90 cm
1 inch	= 2.54 cm
1cm	= 0.39"

Die Grundrezepte lassen sich
in vielfältiger Weise mit den Rezepten
in diesem Buch kombinieren.
Zum Beispiel ist die Rinderbrühe
eine wichtige Zutat vieler Rezepte oder
Spätzle, Knödel oder Apfelmus
sind beliebte Beilagen
der süddeutschen Küche.

The Basic Recipes are used in many
ways in this book.
For example is the beef broth
a basic ingredient for many recipes
and Spaetzle, Bread Dumplings or
Apple Sauce are favorite
side dishes in the
Southern German Kitchen.

Grundrezepte

Basic Recipes

Rinderbrühe

Zutaten:

300 g Suppenknochen vom Rind
500 g Rinderbrust
1 Möhre
¼ Sellerie
½ Kohlrabi
1 Lorbeerblatt
3 Wacholderbeeren
1 Zwiebel
1 Lauchstange
etwas Liebstöckel
frische Petersilie
Salz & Pfefferkörner

Zubereitung:

● Die Knochen mit reichlich kaltem Wasser zum kochen bringen. Suppengrün (Möhre, Sellerie, Lauch, Zwiebel, Kohlrabi, Petersilie und Liebstöckel) sowie Pfefferkörner, Wacholderbeeren und Lorbeerblatt hinzufügen und aufkochen.

● Rinderbrust zugeben und ca. 2 Stunden gar ziehen lassen. Die Brühe von den restlichen Zutaten trennen (durch ein Sieb gießen). Das Fett abschöpfen und mit Salz abschmecken.

● Die Rinderbrust zur weiteren Verwendung herausnehmen.

Homemade Beef Broth

Level
1
Easy

Personen
4
Serves

Zubereitung
5mins
Preparation

Inaktive Zeit
2hrs
Inactive Time

Ingredients:

11 oz. Beef Soup Bones
18 oz. Brisket of Beef
1 Carrot
¼ Knob Celery
½ Kohlrabi (German Turnip)
1 Bay Leaf
3 Juniper Berries
1 Onion
1 Leek
Some Lovage
Fresh Parsley
Salt & Peppercorns

Preparation:

● Bring bones with plenty of cold water to the boil. Add soup-green (carrot, celery, leek, onion, kohlrabi, parsley and lovage) as well as peppercorns, juniper berries and bay leaves then bring to a boil again.

● Now add brisket of beef and let it simmer for approx. 2 hours. Use a strainer to separate the stock from the remaining ingredients. Skim fat from the stock's surface and season to taste with salt.

● Remove the cooked beef from stock for further use.

"Flädle"- Pfannkuchen

German Thin Pancakes

Zutaten:
250 g Weizenmehl
3 Eier
1 TL Salz
375 ml Milch
Öl zum Ausbacken

Zubereitung:

- In einer Rührschüssel die Zutaten mit der Hälfte der Milch zu einem zähflüssigen, glatten Teig verrühren. Nach und nach mit der restlichen Milch verdünnen.
- In einer Pfanne 1 EL Öl erhitzen und 1 Schöpflöffel Teig einfüllen. Pfanne im Kreis schwenken, so dass ein runder, sehr dünner Fladen entsteht.
- Wenn die Teigoberfläche fast trocken ist, wenden und kurz backen. Pfannkuchen auf einem Teller abkühlen lassen.
- Vorgang so oft wiederholen, bis der Teig aufgebraucht ist.

Level
2
Practice

Personen
4
Serves

Zubereitung
15 mins
Preparation

Inaktive Zeit
0 mins
Inactive Time

Ingredients:
2 Cups (9 oz.) Wheat Flour
3 Eggs
1 tsp Salt
1 ½ Cups of Milk
Vegetable Oil for frying

Preparation:
- Put flour, cracked eggs, salt and half of the milk into a mixing bowl. Stir dough and add remaining milk gradually to get a semi fluid, smooth consistency.
- In a pan heat up 1 tbsp of oil, put one soup ladle of dough into the pan. Swivel the pan in a circular motion so that a round, very thin, flat pancake develops.
- When the surface is nearly dry, turn pancake over and briefly bake. Put the pancake on a plate and let cool down slowly.
- Continue until all batter is used.

Pfannkuchen-Variationen

Pfannkuchen mit Marmelade
Pfannkuchen nach Grundrezept herstellen.
Eine Seite mit Marmelade bestreichen und
aufrollen. Mit Puderzucker bestreuen.

Pancakes with Jelly
Prepare Thin Pancakes according to basic recipe.
Spread jelly on one side and roll up.
Dust with Powder Sugar.

Pfannkuchen mit Apfelkompott
Pfannkuchen nach Grundrezept herstellen.
Eine Seite mit Apfelkompott bestreichen und
aufrollen. Mit Puderzucker bestreuen.

Pancakes with Apple Sauce
Prepare Thin Pancakes according to basic recipe.
Spread apple sauce on one side and roll up.
Dust with Powder Sugar.

Pfannkuchen mit Zimt & Zucker
Pfannkuchen nach Grundrezept herstellen.
Zucker mit etwas Zimt mischen, auf einen
Pfannkuchen streuen und aufrollen.

Pancakes with Cinnamon & Sugar
Prepare Thin Pancakes according to basic recipe.
Mix sugar with some cinnamon powder and
sprinkle on pancake. Roll up and enjoy.

Variations for German Pancakes

Pfannkuchen mit Krautern in der Brühe
Rezept Seite 41

Pancakes with Herbs in Broth
Recipe Page 41

Herzhaft gefüllte Pfannkuchen
Rezept Seite 98

Filled Meat-Pancakes
Recipe Page 98

Pfannkuchen mit Spargel
Rezept Seite 105

Pancakes with Asparagus
Recipe Page 105

mit dem Spätzlehobel
with Spätzle Maker

mit der Spätzlepresse
with Spätzle Press

Spätzle

Zutaten:
250g Weizenmehl
6 Eier
1 TL Salz
Wasser & Butter
Spätzlehobel oder -presse (Bild unten)

Zubereitung:
- In einem großen Topf reichlich Wasser mit 1/2 TL Salz zum Kochen bringen.
- Aus Mehl, Salz, Eiern und etwas Wasser einen festen, glatten Teig erstellen, bis er Blasen wirft.
- Den Teig in eine Spätzlepresse geben und die entstehenden Nudeln in das kochende Wasser fallen lassen.
- Sobald die Spätzle wieder an die Oberfläche kommen und das Wasser aufschäumt, die Spätzle mit einem Schaumlöffel abschöpfen. In einem Sieb abtropfen lassen.
- Spätzle in eine Warmhalteform geben und etwas Butter hinzugeben, damit sie nicht zusammenkleben. Im Ofen bei niedriger Temperatur warm halten.
- Machen Sie weiter, bis aller Teig aufgebraucht ist.

Egg-Pasta "Spaetzle"

Level
2
Practice

Personen
4
Serves

Zubereitung
15 mins
Preparation

Inaktive Zeit
0 mins
Inactive Time

Ingredients:
2 Cups (9 oz.) White Whole Wheat Flour
6 Eggs
1 tsp Salt
Some Water & Butter
You will need: Spaetzle Maker or Spaetzle Press (pictured below)

Preparation:
- In a large pot bring water to the boil. Add 1/2 tsp salt.
- Mix flour, eggs, salt and some water into a smooth dough until bubbles start to appear.
- Put a portion of dough into the spaetzle press/maker then force dough through so pieces drop into the boiling water.
- As soon as the spaetzle come back to the surface and the water froths, remove the spaetzle with a skimmer. Put the pasta into a colander and drain.
- Put spaetzle in a (ovenware) casserole dish and add some butter. On very low temperature keep pasta warm in the oven.
- Continue until all dough is used.

Maultaschen

Zutaten Füllung:
500g Hackfleisch
2 Zwiebeln
1 Knoblauchzehe
je ½ Bund Petersilie, Basilikum, Schnittlauch
2 Eier
4 Brötchen vom Vortag, klein geschnitten
Salz, Pfeffer, & Paprika

Zutaten Teig:
500g Weizenmehl
4 Eier
4 Eigelbe
1 TL Salz
1-2 EL Öl

Zubereitung:
- **Teig:** Die Zutaten vermischen und geschmeidig kneten. Eine Arbeitsfläche mit Mehl bestäuben und den Teig dünn auswellen. Die Teigfläche in 10 x 10 cm große Vierecke teilen.
- **Füllung:** Die Brotstücke in Wasser einweichen. Nach ca. 15 min. wieder ausdrücken. Inzwischen die Zwiebel in feine Würfel schneiden und kurz in der Pfanne in Butter anschwitzen. Mit Hackfleisch, der gepressten Knoblauchzehe und gehackten Kräutern zum Brot geben. Eier und Gewürze hinzufügen und alles gut vermengen.
- Die Füllung in passenden Teilen auf den Teigstücken verteilen. Den Rand mit Wasser benetzen. Die Teig-Enden zusammenklappen und fest andrücken.
- Die Maultaschen in reichlich kochendem Salzwasser mit etwas Öl ca. 7-10 Min kochen. Mit einer Schaumkelle heraus nehmen und gut abtropfen lassen. Mit gehacktem Schnittlauch servieren.

Level 3 Challenge

Personen 4 Serves

Zubereitung 35 mins Preparation

Inaktive Zeit 15 mins Inactive Time

Filled Pasta Squares

Filling Ingredients:
18 oz. Ground Meat
2 Onions
1 Clove of Garlic
½ Bunch of each; Parsley, Basil, Chives
2 Eggs
4 Stale Bread Rolls, cut in small pieces
Salt, Pepper, & Paprika

Pasta Dough Ingredients:
18 oz. Wheat Flour
4 Eggs
4 Egg Yolks
1 tsp Salt
1-2 tbsp Vegetable Oil

Preparation:
- **Pasta Dough:** Mix ingredients and knead until smooth. Dust work surface with flour, roll the dough flat with a rolling pin. Cut dough in 4 x 4 inch wide squares.
- **Filling:** Soak bread in water. After 15 mins. squeeze it out. Meanwhile cut onions into small pieces and sweat them in a buttered pan. Mix together with bread, ground meat, minced garlic and chopped herbs, eggs and spices.
- Give a small amount of filling on one side of the rectangles. Moisten edges with water (=glue). Fold dough ends together tightly, so that you get stuffed pasta squares.
- Cook pasta squares for 7-10 minutes in plenty of salted boiling water to which one tablespoon of oil has been added. Use a skimmer to take pasta out and drain well. Sprinkle chopped chives.

Variationen von Spätzle & Maultaschen

Krautspätzle
Spätzle sowie Sauerkraut
nach Grundrezepten herstellen.
Beides mischen und heiß servieren.

Spaetzle with Sauerkraut
Prepare Spaetzle and Sauerkraut
according to the basic recipe.
Mix together and serve hot.

Käsespätzle
Rezept Seite 67

Cheese Noodles
Recipe Page 67

Spinatspätzle mit Mandeln
Spinatspaetzle nach Rezept auf S. 63 zubereiten. 1
Zwiebel würfeln, in Butter glasig dünsten. Spaetzle
und 80 g Mandeln dazugeben und schwenken.

Spinach-Spaetzle with Almonds
Prepare Spinach-Spaetzle according to recipe on pg.
63. Cube 1 Onion and sauté in butter. Add Spaetzle
and 3 oz. Almonds and toss around.

Maultaschen in der Brühe
*Maultaschen sowie Rinderbrühe
nach Grundrezept herstellen.
Maultaschen in der Brühe heiß servieren.*

Filled Pasta Squares in Broth
*Prepare Filled Pasta Squares and Beef Broth
according to basic recipe.
Serve Pasta Squares in hot Broth.*

Gebratene Maultaschen
Rezept Seite 72

Stir-Fried Filled Pasta Squares
Recipe Page 72

Maultaschen mit Spinatfüllung
Rezept Seite 73

Spinach-Filled Pasta Squares
Recipe Page 73

23

Semmelknödel

Zutaten:

6 Brötchen vom Vortag
1 Zwiebel
50 g Räucherspeck
1 EL Margarine
300 ml lauwarme Milch
1 EL zerlassene Butter
4 Eier
2 EL gehackte Petersilie
Salz, Muskat

Zubereitung:

- Die Brötchen klein würfeln und mit lauwarmer Milch übergießen. Ca. 15 min. darin aufquellen lassen.
- Inzwischen Räucherspeck und die Zwiebel in feine Würfel schneiden. In einer Pfanne die Margarine zerlassen. Den Speck knusprig braten und die Zwiebel und Petersilie kurz mitdünsten. Abkühlen lassen.
- In einer großen Schüssel die Eier verquirlen. Die eingeweichten Brötchen, zerlassene Butter, Räucherspeck, Petersilie, eine Prise Salz und etwas Muskatnuss dazugeben und mit den Händen vermischen. Hände immer wieder mit Mehl bestäuben und aus der Masse 12 Klöße formen.
- Wasser mit etwas Salz zum Kochen bringen und die Knödel darin ca. 20 min. gar ziehen lassen (Wasser sollte sich leicht bewegen). Mit einem Schöpflöffel aus dem Wasser nehmen und abtropfen lassen.

Level
2
Practice

Personen
6
Serves

Zubereitung
20 mins
Preparation

Inaktive Zeit
35 mins
Inactive Time

Ingredients:

6 Stale Bread Rolls
1 Onion
2 oz. Smoked Bacon
1 tbsp Margarine
10 fl oz. Milk
1 tbsp melted butter
4 Eggs
2 tbsp Chopped Parsley
Salt, Nutmeg

Preparation:

- Dice Bread Rolls in small cubes. Put with warm Milk in a bowl and set aside for 15 mins.
- Meanwhile cut bacon and onion in small pieces. Heat a pan and melt the margarine in it. Add bacon, onions and parsley and sauté. Let cool down.
- In a big bowl whisk eggs until fluffy. Add bread, bacon, onion, parsley, melted butter, a dash of salt and some nutmeg. Mix with hands to a firm dough. Dust hands with flour and form 12 dumplings.
- Bring salted water to the boil. Drop in dumplings and let them gently simmer for about 20 mins. Then remove with a skimmer and let drain.

Pellkartoffeln

Zutaten:
750 g möglichst gleich große Kartoffeln
kaltes Wasser
1/2 TL Salz

Zubereitung:
Kartoffeln waschen und in einen Topf geben. Dann kaltes Wasser einfüllen, das hoch genug ist, um gerade noch die Kartoffeln zu bedecken. Salz dazugeben und zum Kochen bringen. Den Deckel nur schräg auflegen - nicht schliessen!
Je nach Größe, Kartoffeln ca. 10-20 min. gar kochen lassen. Sie sind fertig, wenn eine Gabel sich bis zur Mitte leicht einstechen lässt. Die Kartoffeln abgießen und warm servieren.

Boiled Potatoes

Level
1
Easy

Personen
4
Serves

Zubereitung
5 mins
Preparation

Inaktive Zeit
20 mins
Inactive Time

Ingredients:
26 oz. Potatoes, about the same size
Cold Water
1/2 tsp Salt

Preparation:
Rinse potatoes under water. Put them in a pot and cover with cold water until the potatoes are just submerged. Add salt. Then turn on the heat and bring the water to a boil. Put lid not completely on! Leave room to let off steam.
Cook potatoes for about 10-20 mins depending on size. Your potatoes are done when you encounter no resistance all the way through the center by poking them with a fork. Drain and serve warm.

Bratkartoffeln

Zutaten:
750 g Pellkartoffeln
1 kleine Zwiebel
3 Scheiben Räucherspeck
1 EL Butter zum Braten
Salz, Pfeffer

Zubereitung:
Die Pellkartoffeln von der Schale befreien. Kartoffeln in Viertel oder Scheiben schneiden. Die Zwiebel in feinste Würfel schneiden. Den Räucherspeck zuerst in feine Streifen längs, dann quer schneiden.
In einer Pfanne die Butter zerlassen und die Zwiebel mit dem Speck darin anbraten. Die Kartoffeln dazugeben und kurz darin schwenken. Mit Salz und Pfeffer bestreuen. Nicht ständig rühren. Nur vorsichtig die Kartoffeln wenden und braun anbraten. Heiß servieren.

Frühstücksvariante: Die Bratkartoffeln mit einer Eiermilch aus 3 Eiern und etwas Milch, Paprika und geriebener Muskatnuss übergießen. Die Eiermilch stocken lassen und einmal wenden.

Roasted Potatoes

Level
1
Easy

Personen
4
Serves

Zubereitung
10 mins
Preparation

Inaktive Zeit
0 mins
Inactive Time

Ingredients:
26 oz. Boiled Potatoes
1 Small Onion
2 Slices Smoked Bacon
1 tbsp Butter for frying
Salt, Pepper

Preparation:
Peel skin off the potatoes. Cut potatoes into quaters or slice them. Cut the onion finely into cubes. Slice bacon into thin strips lengthways then across.
In a skillet melt the butter and sauté onions and bacon. Add potatoes and toss quickly. Then add salt and pepper. Do not stir. Just let potatoes brown nicely and then gently turn around. Serve hot.

Breakfast Variation: Pour 3 whisked eggs with some milk over roasted potatoes. Season with nutmeg and paprika powder. When eggs have thickened, flip over.

Sauerkraut

Grundzutaten:
5 kg frisch gehobeltes Weisskraut
70 g Salz (entspricht ca. 1,4 % des Kohls)
5 L Gärtopf oder 5 x 1 L Einweckgläser
Essig zum Auswaschen

Optionale Zutaten:
2 EL Wachholderbeeren
40 g Kümmel
500 g grob geraspelte Möhren

Zubereitung:
- Von den Weisskohlköpfen die äußeren Blätter und den Strunk entfernen. Anschließend wird der Kohl fein gehobelt. Kohl mit Salz mischen ca. 3/4 in einen Gärtopf bzw. in Einweckgläser einfüllen und ordentlich einstampfen bis Saft entsteht und dieser das Kraut bedeckt. Den Deckel schließen.
- Das Kraut sollte für mindestens ca. 14 Tage an einem warmen Ort zum Gären stehen gelassen werden (evtl. kann etwas Flüssigkeit auslaufen). Danach soll der Topf in einen kühleren Raum bei ca. 15° C gebracht werden, um die Haltbarkeit zu verlängern.
- Nach 14 Tagen schmeckt das Kraut schon sauer. Nach spätestens 1 Monat ist das Sauerkraut fertig zum Essen. Bei Verwendung eines Gärtopfes die Rinne immer mit Wasser oder Essig füllen, dann bildet sich kein Schimmel im Topf.

Sauerkraut: Fermented Cabbage

Level
1
Easy

Menge
5 L
Amount

Zubereitung
30 mins
Preparation

Inaktive Zeit
1
Monat/Month
Inactive Time

Basic Ingredients:
175 oz. Freshly Shredded White Cabbage,
3 oz. Salt (approx. 1.4 % of cabbage)
1,3 gal Fermenting Crock Pot
or 5 x 34 fl. oz. jars for food preservation

Optional Ingredients:
2 tbsp Juniper Berries
1 1/2 oz. Caraway Seeds
18 oz. Coarsely Shredded Carrots

Preparation:
- Remove the wilting outer leaves and the stalk of the cabagge. Finely shredd cabbage with a handheld slicer. Mix cabbage with salt and fill 3/4 of the crock or jars with cabbage. Then knead or pulp cabbage to break it down and liquid comes out. The liquid should cover the cabbage completely. Close lid.
- Let crock or jars rest at a warm place to start the fermentation (maybe some liquid could overflow). Then store at a cooler place at about 60° F to extend preservability.
- After 14 days the cabbage will taste sour. But it needs about 1 month to complete fermentation and the cabbage is ready to eat. If you use a crock, make sure that the channel has enough water or vinegar to avoid mold.

Variationen für Kohl

Gebackenes Kraut mit Weinschaum
Rezept Seite 59

Kraut Bake with Wine Sauce
Recipe Page 59

Krautsalat
Rezept Seite 57

German Coleslaw
Recipe Page 57

Kohlrouladen
Rezept Seite 106

Cabbage Rolls
Recipe Page 106

Variations for Cabbage

Schupfnudeln mit Sauerkraut
Rezept Seite 71

Schupfnudeln with Sauerkraut
Recipe Page 71

Kartoffel-Striezel mit Kraut
Rezept Seite 69

Potato Striezel with Sauerkraut
Recipe Page 69

Nürnberger Würste mit Sauerkraut
Rezept Seite 95

Nuremberg Sausages with Kraut
Recipe Page 95

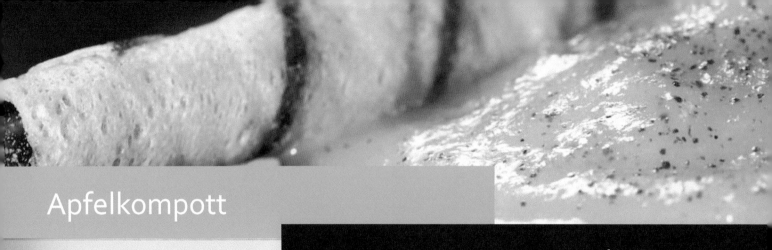

Apfelkompott

Zutaten:
750 g Äpfel (z.B. Boskoop)
500 ml Wasser
3-4 EL Zucker
1 Zimtstange oder Zitronenschale

Zubereitung:
Wasser, Zucker und Zimt oder Zitronenschale zusammen aufkochen. Äpfel waschen, vierteln und entkernen. In das kochende Wasser geben, das inzwischen den Geschmack der Gewürze angenommen hat.

Bei schwacher Hitze und zugedeckt die Äpfel weich und glasig kochen (etwa 10-15 Min.).

Einen Topf mit grobem Sieb bereithalten. Die Äpfel durch das Sieb in das gekochte Zuckerwasser passieren (zerstampfen).

Mit Zucker und Zimt abschmecken.

Apfelkompott passt gut zu:
- *Pfannkuchen S. 16*
- *Kaiserschmarren S. 121*
- *Dampfnudeln S. 126*
- *Biskuitwaffeln S. 131*

Apple Sauce

Level **1** Easy	
Personen **4** Serves	
Zubereitung **15** mins Preparation	
Inaktive Zeit **15** mins Inactive Time	

Ingredients:
26 oz. Apples (e.g. Boskoop)
2 cups of Water
3-4 tbsp Sugar
1 Cinnamon Stick or Lemon Zest

Preparation:
- Bring water to boil with sugar and cinnamon stick. Rinse apples under water, quarter and core them. Put them into the seasoned boiling water. Reduce heat and cover with a lid.
- Let apples simmer for 10-15 minutes until they are translucent and soft.
- Drain the apples into a second pot with a coarse sieve on top. Remove the cinnamon stick then puree the apples by pressing them through the sieve into the cooked sugar-water.
- Season to taste with sugar and cinnamon.

Apple Sauce goes well with:
- *German Pancakes p. 16*
- *Fluffy Scratched Pancake p. 121*
- *Yeast Dumplings p. 126*
- *Biscuit Waffles p. 131*

Zwetschgenkompott

Damson Sauce

Zutaten:
750 g Hauszwetschgen
(oder andere Pflaumenarten)
250 ml Wasser
60 g Zucker
1 Zimtstange

Zubereitung:
Zwetschgen im Zuckerwasser mit der Zimtstange
weich kochen.
Zimtstange entfernen.
● Die Hälfte der Zwetschgen durch ein Sieb in
das Zuckerwasser passieren (zerstampfen).
● Die andere Hälfte dem Püree untermischen.
● Mit wenig Zucker und Zimt abschmecken.

*Pflaumenmus passt besonders gut zum
Kaiserschmarren S. 121.*

Level
1
Easy

Personen
4
Serves

Zubereitung
15 mins
Preparation

Inaktive Zeit
15 mins
Inactive Time

Ingredients:
26 oz. Damsons (or other plums)
1 cup of Water
2 oz. Sugar
1 Cinnamon Stick

Preparation:
● Cook the cleaned, halved and pitted damsons
in sugared cinnamon-water until they are soft.
Drain the damsons into a second pot with a
sieve on top.
● Remove the cinnamon stick.
● Puree half of the damsons by pressing them
through the sieve into the sugar-water.
● Add the other damsons to the puree.
● Season to taste with sugar and cinnamon.

*Damson Sauce goes very well with the
Fluffy Scratched Pancake p. 121.*

Holundermus

Elder Sauce

Zutaten:

500 g reife schwarze Holunderbeeren
150 g Zucker
250 ml Milch
2-3 EL Mehl
Butter

Zubereitung:

- Holunderbeeren, Zucker und Milch zum Kochen bringen. Mindestens 4 Min. bei 80°C kochen ansonsten können die Beeren gesundheitliche Probleme bereiten.
- Inzwischen das Mehl mit etwas kalter Milch anrühren, in die kochende Masse einrühren und mitkochen, damit das Mus gebunden wird.
- Zum Schluss mit etwas Butter abschmecken.

Das Holundermus passt gut zu Schnecken-nudeln S. 124 oder zu Biskuitwaffeln S. 131.

Level
1
Easy

Personen
4
Serves

Zubereitung
15 mins
Preparation

Inaktive Zeit
0 mins
Inactive Time

Ingredients:

26 oz. Elderberries
6 oz. Sugar
8 fl oz. Milk
2-3 tbsp Flour
Butter

Preparation:

- Bring elderberries, sugar and milk to the boil. Let it boil at least 4 min. at 180°F, otherwise the berries will cause health problems.
- Meanwhile, mix the flour with some cold milk to avoid lumps. Then pour it into the boiling liquid to thicken the sauce. Stir well.
- Finally, season to taste with some butter.

The Elder Sauce goes well with Sweet Spiral Yeast Noodles or with Biscuit Waffles p. 131.

Rumtopf mit Kirschen

Zutaten:
1 kg Frische Sauer-Kirschen
500 g Feiner Zucker
Echter Rum (mind. 54% Alkohol)
Rumtopf mit dicht schließendem Deckel

Zubereitung:
Kirschen entsteinen und in den Rumtopf geben. Mit dem Zucker bedecken und ca. 1 Stunde einwirken lassen.

Alles mit Rum übergießen. Der Rum sollte einen Fingerbreit über den Früchten stehen. Die Kirschen mit einem Teller beschweren (sonst Schimmelgefahr).

Den Rumtopf mit dem Deckel verschließen und dunkel lagern. In den nächsten 6 Wochen immer wieder umrühren, wieder Teller drauf und mit Deckel luftdicht verschließen.

Die Kirschen passen gut zu:
- *Vanilleeis mit heissen Kirschen*
- *Biskuitwaffeln S. 131*
- *Schwarzwaldbecher S. 133*
- *Donauwellen S. 155*
- *Biskuit Rolle S. 161*
- *Schwarzwälder Kirschtorte S. 162*

Level
1
Easy

Personen
10
Serves

Zubereitung
15 mins
Preparation

Inaktive Zeit
1 hr
+ 6 weeks/ Wochen
Inactive Time

Rum Pot with Cherries

Ingredients:
35 oz. Fresh Sour Cherries
18 oz. Fine Sugar
Real Rum (min. 54% alcohol)
Rum Pot with a tightly closing lid on it

Preparation:
- First pit the cherries and put them in the rum pot. Cover them with sugar and allow to stand for one hour.
- Cover everything with the rum, so that more than ½ inch of the liquid is on top of the cherries. Ballast the cherries with a plate, so that they cannot swim to the surface in order to avoid them to get moldy.
- Seal the rum pot with the lid and store in a dark place. Within the following 6 weeks stir from time to time, recover cherries with the plate and seal the pot.

The Cherries are going well with:
- *Vanilla Ice Cream & Hot Cherries*
- *Biscuit Waffles p. 131*
- *Black Forest Cup p. 133*
- *Danubian Waves p. 155*
- *Biscuit Roll p. 161*
- *Black Forest Cake p. 162*

Aprikosenknödel S. 128
Apricot Dumplings p. 128

Ofenschlupfer S. 123
Bread Bake p. 123

Dampfnudeln S. 126
Yeast Dumplings p. 126

Bratapfel S. 135
Bakes Apple p. 135

Apfelstrudel S. 139
Apple Strudel p. 139

Vanillesoße

Zutaten:
500 ml Milch
1 Vanilleschote
1 Pkg. Vanillezucker
3 Eigelb
3 EL Zucker
2 EL Speisestärke

Zubereitung:
- In einer Schüssel die Eigelbe zusammen mit dem Zucker, Vanillezucker und Speisestärke schaumig rühren.
- Die Vanilleschote der Länge nach aufschneiden. Das Mark (schwarze, ölige Samen) aus der Vanilleschote kratzen. Das Vanillemark, Vailleschote und Milch in einem Topf erhitzen und einmal aufkochen lassen. Dann die
- Hitze reduzieren. Die Vanilleschote herausnehmen.
  Die Ei-Mixtur zur Vanille-Milch hinzugeben und mit einem Schneebesen solange verquirlen, bis die Vanillesoße cremig ist (nicht aufkochen!).
- Noch warm zu Süßspeisen servieren.

Vanilla Sauce

Level
1
Easy

Personen
4
Serves

Zubereitung
10 mins
Preparation

Inaktive Zeit
0 mins
Inactive Time

Ingredients:
17 fl oz. Milk
1 Vanilla Bean
1 Pkg. (0.35 oz.) Vanilla Sugar
3 Egg Yolk
3 tbsp Sugar
2 tbsp Cornstarch

Preparation:
- In a bowl whisk eggs, sugar, vailla sugar and cornstarch together until fluffy.
- Pour milk into a pot. Slit the vanilla pod open along its length, then scrape out the small, sticky seeds using the tip of a small, sharp knife. Add the seeds to the milk together with the vanilla pod. Bring to the boil. Then remove pod and reduce heat.
- Pour in egg-mixture into vanilla-milk and whisk until the sauce becomes creamy. Do not bring it to the boil.
- Serve warm to dumplings, strudel and cake.

Linke Seite: Hier ein paar leckere Rezepte, zu denen Vanillesoße passt!
Left Page: Here are some delicious recipes that goes well with Vanilla Sauce!

Suppen & Salate

Soups & Salads

Broth with Herbal Pancakes

Zutaten Pfannkuchen:
250 g Weizenmehl
3 Eier
1 TL Salz
375 ml Milch
Öl zum Ausbacken
1 kleine Zwiebel
2 EL Küchenkräuter (Schnittlauch, Petersilie, Basilikum)

Zutaten Rindfleischbrühe:
1 L Rindfleischbrühe (siehe Grundrezept oder 1 Liter Wasser mit entsprechender Menge an Fleischbrühwürfeln vorbereiten)

Zubereitung:
- Die Zwiebel in kleinste Würfel schneiden und in etwas Fett anschwitzen. Bei Seite stellen und abkühlen lassen.
- Aus den restlichen Zutaten einen Pfannkuchenteig herstellen (siehe Grundrezept), dabei zuletzt Kräuter und gedünstete Zwiebeln untermischen.
- In einer Pfanne etwas Pflanzenöl erhitzen und einen Schöpflöffel Teig darin verteilen. Die Pfanne rund schwenken, sodaß der Teig dünn und flach ist. Wenn der Teig Blasen wirft, wenden und kurz anbraten. Auf ein Schneidebrett geben.
- Nach dem Abkühlen eng aufrollen und quer in dünne Streifen schneiden. Den Teig aufbrauchen.
- Rindfleischbrühe erhitzen und Flädlestreifen in der heißen Brühe servieren.

Level
2
Practice

Personen
4
Serves

Zubereitung
25 mins
Preparation

Inaktive Zeit
0 mins
Inactive Time

Ingredients Pancakes:
2 Cups (9 oz.) Wheat Flour
3 Eggs
1 tsp Salt
1 ½ Cups of Milk
1 small Onion
2 tbsp Kitchen Herbs (chives, parsley, basil)

Ingredients Beef Broth:
1 qt Beef Broth (see Basic Recipes or prepare 1 qt Water with corresponding amount of Buillon Cubes)

Preparation:
- Finely chopp onion. Braise lightly in buttered pan. Set aside for cooling.
- Prepare a pancake batter with other ingredients (see basic recipe). Add chopped herbs and onions to the batter and mix well.
- In a pan heat some vegetable oil. Add about one dipper of batter and sway the pan a little until the batter is flat and round. Wait until surface is bubbly and nearly dry and toss the pancake. Bake shortly on this side. Put on cutting board to cool down.
- Roll up pancake tightly and cut across into thin strips. Repeat steps untill all batter has been used.
- Bring beef broth to the boil and serve with pancake strips.

Speckknödelsuppe

Bacon-Dumpling Soup

Zutaten Knödel:
8 Brötchen vom Vortag
1 Zwiebel
100 g Räucherspeck
50 g Salami
1 EL Margarine
250 ml lauwarme Milch
1 EL zerlassene Butter
3 Eier
2 EL gehackte Petersilie
2 EL gehackter Schnittlauch
1 Knoblauchzehe
Salz, Pfeffer, Muskat

Zutaten Rindfleischbrühe:
1 L Rindfleischbrühe (siehe Grundrezept-oder 1 Liter Wasser mit entsprechender Menge an Fleischbrühwürfeln vorbereiten)

Zubereitung:
● Die oben genannten Zutaten für die Knödel entsprechend dem Grundrezept anfertigen. Zuletzt fein gewürfelte Salami, gehackter Knoblauch, Schnittlauch und Mehl hinzufügen. Mit den Gewürzen abschmecken.
● Die Masse zu einem festen Teig formen und daraus gleichmäßig große Knödel formen.
● Die Fleischbrühe erhitzen und die Knödel darin gar ziehen lassen (ca. 15 Min).
● Pro Suppenteller 3-4 Knödel mit Brühe einfüllen und mit etwas gehacktem Schnittlauch servieren.

Level
2
Practice

Personen
6
Serves

Zubereitung
20 mins
Preparation

Inaktive Zeit
20 mins
Inactive Time

Ingredients:
8 Stale Bread Rolls
1 Onion
4 oz. Smoked Bacon
2 oz. Salami
1 tbsp Margarine
8 fl oz. Milk
1 tbsp melted butter
3 Eggs
2 tbsp Chopped Parsley
2 tbsp Chopped Chives
1 Garlic Clove
Salt, Pepper, Nutmeg

Ingredients Beef Broth:
1 qt Beef Broth (see Basic Recipes or prepare 1 qt Water with corresponding amount of Buillon Cubes)

Preparation:
● Prepare Dumplings with the above-named ingredients according to the Basic Recipe. In a final step add finely diced salami, chopped garlic, chives and flour. Season with spices.
● Use your hands to mix all ingredients to a firm dough. If the dough is still too soft, add more flour. Then form dumplings.
● Bring the broth to boil. Reduce the heat, put in the dumplings and let them simmer for about 15 mins until the dumplings are soft and ready to eat.
● Fill each plate with 3-4 dumplings and broth. Serve with chopped chives.

Leberknödel Suppe

Zutaten:

300 g Rinderleber-Hack
1 Zwiebel
1 Knoblauchzehe
3 Brötchen vom Vortag
3 Eier
250 ml lauwarme Milch
Salz, Pfeffer, Majoran, Muskatnuss
1 EL gehackte Petersilie
3 EL Mehl
1 L Fleischbrühe

Zubereitung:

- Die Zwiebel sowie Knoblauch fein hacken.
- Die Brötchen in kleine Würfel schneiden.
- In einer großen Schüssel die Eier verquirlen. Die Gewürze, frische Petersilie, Zwiebeln, Knoblauch dazugeben und vermischen. Dann das Leber-Hack, Brötchenstücke, Mehl und die Milch hinzugeben und alles gut vermischen.
- Die Zutaten in der abgedeckten Schüssel ca. 1 Stunde quellen lassen.
- Aus dem Teig 8 gleich große Knödel formen. Diese in die schwach strudelnden Fleischbrühe einlegen und ca. 30 min. zugedeckt ziehen lassen.
- In der heißen Fleischbrühe oder als Beilage zum Sauerkraut servieren.

Level
1
Easy

Personen
4
Serves

Zubereitung
20 mins
Preparation

Inaktive Zeit
90 mins
Inactive Time

Liver-Dumpling Soup

Ingredients:

11 oz. Ground Liver of Beef
1 Onion
1 Garlic Clove
3 Stale Breads Rolls
3 Eggs
8 fl oz. Lukewarm Milk
Salt, Pepper, Marjoram, Nutmeg
1 tbsp Chopped Parsley
3 tbsp Flour
34 fl oz. Bouillon

Preparation:

- Chopp finely onion and garlic.
- Dice the bread rolls into small cubes.
- In a bowl whisk eggs until fluffy. Add spices, fresh parsley, onion and garlic and mix well. Then add ground liver, bread cubes, flour and milk and mix together.
- Set bowl covered for about 1 hour aside, so that the ingredients can soak nicely.
- Form 8 dumplings from the dough. Gently put them into the lightly whirling bouillon and let dumplings simmer for about 30 mins.
- Serve hot dumplings together with the bouillon or as a side dish with sauerkraut.

Kartoffel-Möhren Suppe

Zutaten:

750 g mehlig kochende Kartoffeln
4 Möhren
1 Lauchstange
1 Kleine Sellerieknolle
1 Kleine Zwiebel
1,5 L Wasser
Salz & Pfeffer
Butter zum Anbraten

Zubereitung:

- Das Gemüse von der Schale befreien, säubern und in kleinere Stücke schneiden. In einem Topf die Butter erhitzen und darin das Gemüse andünsten (niedrige Temperatur). Mit Wasser aufgießen und alles weich kochen.
- Einen anderen Topf bereithalten. Durch ein Sieb das Gemüse vom Wasser trennen, das im anderen Topf aufgefangen wird. Das Gemüse durch das Sieb passieren oder durch eine Presse drücken. Etwas Gemüsewasser zugeben.
- Die Suppe nochmals erhitzen und bei niedriger Temperatur etwas eindicken lassen. Mit Salz und Pfeffer abschmecken.

Variante: Zuletzt etwas klein gewürfeltes Rauchfleisch oder dünne Parmaschinken-Streifen zugeben.

Potato-Carrot Soup

Level
1
Easy

Personen
4
Serves

Zubereitung
15 mins
Preparation

Inaktive Zeit
30 mins
Inactive Time

Ingredients:

26 oz. Floury Potatoes
4 Carrots
1 Leek
1 Small Celery Corm
1 Small Onion
1 ½ qt Water
Salt & Pepper
Butter for frying

Preparation:

- Peel vegetables, rinse under water and cut into small pieces. Melt the butter in a large pot, add vegetables and sauté on low temperature. Add water and simmer vegetables under reduced heat, until soft.
- Using a second pot and a sieve; strain vegetables through the sieve and catch the vegetable water in the second pot. Press the vegetables through the sieve to puree or use a vegetable press (or a spaetzle press). Add some vegetable water.
- Put vegetable water together with the vegetable puree and reheat. Reduce heat to let it simmer for a while and thicken. Season to taste with salt and pepper.

Variation: You can also add diced smoked meat or small cubes of Parma ham.

Schwäbischer Kartoffelsalat

Swabian Potato Salad

Zutaten:
1 kg fest kochende Kartoffeln
1 Mittelgroße Zwiebel
250 ml Kräftige Fleischbrühe
1-2 TL Mittelscharfer Senf
2-3 EL Obst- oder Weinessig
2-3 EL Sonnenblumenöl
Salz, Pfeffer aus der Mühle und etwas
Schnittlauch

Zubereitung:
- Im Dampftopf die Kartoffeln mit Schale in etwas Salzwasser weich kochen (ca. 7-10 min.). Dann das Wasser abgießen und die Kartoffeln leicht auskühlen lassen. Die noch leicht warme Kartoffel mit einer Kuchengabel aufnehmen und mit einem kleinen Küchenmesser die Schale abziehen.
- Die abgezogenen Kartoffeln in ca. 3mm dicke Scheiben schneiden und in eine Salatschüssel geben.
- Die Zwiebel schälen und in feine Würfel schneiden.
- Die Fleischbrühe erwärmen.
- Die Zwiebel, Salz und Pfeffer sowie den Senf großflächig darüber verteilen. Dann den Essig und die Fleischbrühe aufgießen. Alles vorsichtig mit einem großen Löffel gut vermengen.
- Ca. 15 min. im Kühlschrank abgedeckt ruhen lassen.
- Zuletzt das Öl zugeben und nochmals mit Essig, Salz und Pfeffer abschmecken. Evtl. mit gehacktem Schnittlauch anrichten.

Level
1
Easy

Personen
4
Serves

Zubereitung
15 mins
Preparation

Inaktive Zeit
25 mins
Inactive Time

Ingredients:
35 oz. Waxy Potatoes
1 Middle Sized Onion
8 fl oz. Beef or Chicken Stock
1-2 tsp Medium Hot Mustard
2-3 tbsp Fruit or Wine Vinegar
2-3 tbsp Sun Flower Oil
Salt, Ground Pepper & Chopped Chives

Preparation:
- Put potatoes in a pressure cooker with some salted water. Bring water to a boil. Close pot with lid. Reduce heat and let the potatoes simmer for about 7-10 mins until a fork can easily pierce the potato. Pour off water and let potatoes cool down. Pick up hand-warm potato with a small fork and peel off skin with a small paring knife.
- Slice the peeled potatoes about 1/8 inch thick into a salad bowl.
- Meanwhile peel the onion and cut it in small pieces.
- Reheat the stock.
- Spread onion, salt, pepper and mustard over the entire surface of potatoes. Carefully mingle with a large spoon. Step by step, add vinegar and stock so the potatoes can absorb the liquid.
- Put aside in fridge for about 15min.
- Finally add oil then again season to taste with vinegar, salt and pepper. Serve with copped chives on top.

Apfel-Möhren Salat

Zutaten:

600 g Möhren
400 g Äpfel
5-6 EL Zitronensaft
4 EL Öl
4 EL Wasser
Salz
Etwas Zucker
Optional: 1 EL gehackte Haselnüsse

Zubereitung:

● Die Möhren waschen und ggf. schälen. Auf einer Reibe in eine Schüssel raspeln. Danach die Äpfel waschen, schälen, vierteln und vom Kerngehäuse befreien. Ebenfalls auf der Reibe in die Schüssel raspeln.

● Sofort mit Zitronensaft übergießen, damit die Äpfel nicht braun werden.

● Dann das Öl, Wasser, Salz und etwas Zucker hinzugeben und mit der Rohkost vermischen.

● Je nach Belieben den vitaminreichen Salat mit gehackten Haselnüssen anreichern.

Apple-Carrot Salad

Level
1
Easy

Personen
4
Serves

Zubereitung
15 mins
Preparation

Inaktive Zeit
0 mins
Inactive Time

Ingredients:

22 oz. Carrots
14 oz. Apples
5-6 tbsp Freshly Squeezed Lemon Juice
4 tbsp Vegetable Oil
4 tbsp Water
Salt
Some Sugar
Optionally + 1 tbsp Ground Hazelnuts

Preparation:

● Rinse the carrots, peel as necessary then grate them. Rinse, peel, quarter and core the apples. Grate them too.

● Immediately dribble apples with lemon juice to keep them from turning brown.

● Add oil, water, salt, sugar and mix gently.

● If you like, add some coarsely ground hazelnuts to this vitamin-packed salad.

Pikanter Wurstsalat

Zutaten:
500 g gerauchte Schinkenwurst
1 Große Zwiebel
4 Kleine Essiggurken
½ TL Senf
5 EL Apfelessig
3 EL Wasser
5 EL Sonnenblumenöl
Salz, weißer Pfeffer aus der Mühle

Zubereitung:
- Die Schinkenwurst in feine Streifen oder Scheiben schneiden. Die Zwiebel häuten und in dünne Zwiebelringe schneiden. Essiggurken gut abtropfen lassen und in feine Streifen schneiden.
- Aus Essig, Öl, Wasser, Senf, einer Prise Salz und frischem Pfeffer aus der Mühle eine pikante Salatsoße zubereiten.
- Die Salatsoße mit der Wurst, Zwiebel und den Essiggurken mischen und gut 1 Stunde zugedeckt im Kühlschrank ziehen lassen.
- Dazu reicht man ein Glas frisch gezapftes Bier und ofenwarmes Bauernbrot.

Variante 1: 300 g Schinkenwurst und 200 g Schwarzwurst (Blutwurst) verwenden.

Variante 2: 300 g Schinkenwurst und 200 g Gouda Käse verwenden.

Savoury Sausage Salad

Level
1
Easy

Personen
4
Serves

Zubereitung
15 mins
Preparation

Inaktive Zeit
1 hrs
Inactive Time

Ingredients:
18 oz. Smoked Ham Sausage
1 Large Onion
4 Small Gherkins
½ tsp Mustard
5 tbsp Cider Vinegar
3 tbsp Water
5 tbsp Sunflower Oil
Salt, freshly ground White Pepper

Preparation:
- Slice ham sausage in thin slices or rings. Peel onion and cut it in thin, onion rings. Drain the gherkins and cut into slices ¼ inch thick.
- For the dressing, mix vinegar, oil, water, mustard, a pinch of salt and white pepper.
- Mingle ham sausage, onion, gherkins and dressing well. Cover bowl well and put into the fridge for at least 1 hour.
- Serve with draught beer and homemade warm farmers' bread.

Variation 1: Use 11 oz. Ham Sausage and 8 oz. Blood Sausage.

Variation 2: Use 11 oz. Ham Sausage and 8 oz. Gouda Cheese.

Feldsalat mit Erdbeeren

Zutaten:

250 g Feldsalat
1/2 Bund Frischer Basilikum
500 g Erdbeeren
50 g Schafskäse
5 EL Aceto Balsamico
50 g Honig
8 EL Sonnenblumen- oder Olivenöl
4 EL Walnüsse, geröstet
Salz, Pfeffer

Zubereitung:

● Den Feldsalat von den Wurzeln befreien, waschen und gut abtropfen lassen.

● Den Schafskäse in kleine Stücke zerteilen.

● Basilikum grob zerkleinern.

● Aus dem Balsamico, dem Honig, Salz und Pfeffer sowie dem Öl eine Salatsoße herstellen.

● Die Erdbeeren waschen und halbieren.

● Auf einer Servierplatte den Feldsalat anrichten und mit Basilikum bestreuen. Mit Erdbeeren belegen. Alles mit der Salatsoße beträufeln. Dann den Schafskäse und die Walnüsse darauf verteilen.

Nut Lettuce with Strawberries

Level
1
Easy

Personen
4
Serves

Zubereitung
10 mins
Preparation

Inaktive Zeit
0 mins
Inactive Time

Ingredients:

9 oz. Nut Lettuce (also called: Corn Salad, Mache, Lamb's Lettuce)
1/2 Bunch of Fresh Basil
18 oz. Strawberries
2 oz. Sheep's Cheese
5 tbsp Balsamic Vinegar
2 fl. oz. Honey
8 tbsp Sunflower- or Olive Oil
4 tbsp Roasted Walnuts
Salt, Pepper

Preparation:

● Rinse the lettuce, sort carefully and drain well.

● Cut the cheese in small pieces.

● Chopp the basil.

● In a small bowl prepare a salad sauce from balsamic vinegar, honey, salt, pepper and oil.

● Rinse and drain strawberries and cut in haves.

● On a serving plate arrange lettuce with basil and strawberries and drizzle with the salad sauce. Sprinkle with cheese and walnuts.

Einfacher Krautsalat

Zutaten:
1 kg Weißkohl
1 EL Salz
1 EL Zucker
100 ml Rapsöl
150 ml Essig

Zubereitung:
● Äußere Blätter entfernen, Kopf vierteln, Strunk entfernen und mit einem Gemüsehobel fein hobeln. Salz darüber streuen und mit der Hand ca. 4 min. durch durchkneten.
● Essig, Zucker und das Öl in einem Topf erhitzen, jedoch nicht zum Kochen bringen. Die Zutaten auf das Kraut geben und gut durchmischen.
● In den Kühlschrank geben und mindestens 2 Stunden ziehen lassen, besser über Nacht.

German Coleslaw

Level
1
Easy

Personen
4
Serves

Zubereitung
20 mins
Preparation

Inaktive Zeit
2 hrs
Inactive Time

Ingredients:
35 oz. White Cabbage
1 tbsp Salt
1 tbsp Sugar
3 1/2 fl.oz. Canola Oil
5 fl. oz. Vinegar

Preparation:
● Remove the wilting outer leaves and the stalk of the cabagge. Finely shredd cabbage with a handheld slicer. Mix cabbage with salt and knead with hands for about 4 mins.
● In a pot warm up vinegar with sugar and oil. do not bring to the boil. Mix warm ingredients with cabbage.
● Put into refrigerator for at least 2 hours, better over night.

Kraut in Weinsoße

Zutaten:
1/2 Weißkohl
1/2 Rotkohl
2 EL Pflanzenöl
Salz, Pfeffer
1/8 L Weißwein
1/8 L Wasser
1/2 TL getrockneter Koriander
1/2 TL getrockneter Thymian
1/8 L Sahne
3 EL Apfelsaft
1-2 EL Mehl

Zubereitung:
- Den Backofen auf 220°C vorheizen.
- Äußere Blätter des Krautkopfes entfernen, Strunk entfernen. Krautkopfhälften in achtel schneiden.
- In einer feuerfesten Form die Krautstücke rundherum mit Öl einreiben. Die Krautstücke gleichmäßig in der Form verteilen und mit Salz, Pfeffer, Koriander und Thymian würzen. Wein mit Wasser mischen und über das Kraut gießen.
- Die Form zudecken und ca. 35 Minuten im Backofen garen lassen.
- Danach die Flüssigkeit in einen Topf gießen und die Sahne dazugeben. Alles aufkochen lassen. Das Mehl in einer Tasse mit dem Apfelsaft anrühren und die Soße damit binden. Mit Salz und Pfeffer abschmecken.
- Die Soße über das Kraut gießen und heiß servieren.

Cabbage in Wine Sauce

Level
1
Easy

Personen
4
Serves

Zubereitung
10 mins
Preparation

Inaktive Zeit
35 mins
Inactive Time

Ingredients:
1/2 White Cabbage
1/2 Red Cabbage
2 tbsp Vegatable Oil
Salt, Pepper
4 fl oz. White Wine
4 fl oz. Water
1/2 tsp Dried Cilantro
1/2 tsp Dried Thyme
4 fl oz. Cream
3 tbsp Apple Juice
1-2 tbsp Flour

Preparation:
- Preheat oven to 425° F.
- Remove the wilting outer leaves and the stalk of the cabagge. Cut cabbage halves into eights.
- Place cabbage into an ovenproof dish and coat with Oil. Layer cabbage evenly in dish. Then season with salt, pepper, cilantro and thyme. Mix wine with water and pour over cabbage.
- Cover dish with lid or tinfoil and put in the oven. Let cabbage cook for about 35 mins.
- After that pour liquid into a pot. Add cream and heat. In a cup mix apple juice with flour and thicken wine-cream-sauce with it. Season to taste with salt and pepper.
- Pour sauce over cabbage and serve hot.

Nudeln & Kartoffel- gerichte

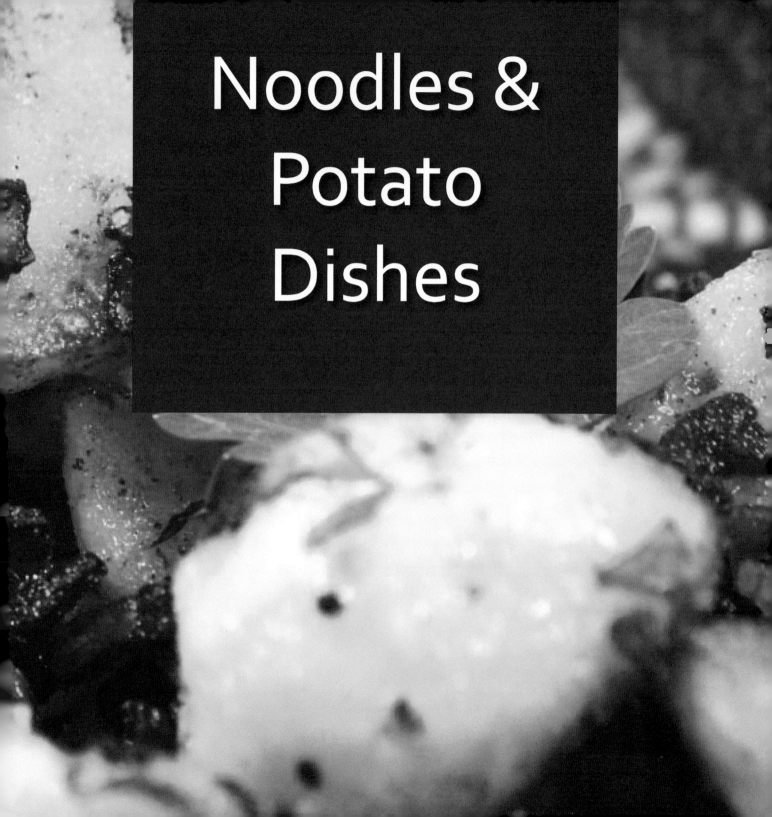

Noodles & Potato Dishes

Spinatspätzle-Auflauf

Zutaten Spätzlesteig:
250 g Mehl
4 Eier
1 TL Salz
4 EL fein gehackter Spinat

Zutaten Auflauf:
1 Becher Crème fraiche
5 Steinchampignons
5 Weiße Champignons
½ Zwiebel
1 Stange Lauch
Salz, Pfeffer aus der Mühle
150 g Geriebener Gouda

Zubereitung:
- Für den Spätzlesteigs die Zutaten mischen und zu einem ziehbaren Teig verkneten (siehe Grundrezept).
- Salzwasser zum Kochen bringen. Mit einem Spätzleshobel den Teig portionsweise ins Wasser reiben. Kurz aufkochen lassen (es muss schäumen), herausnehmen, gut abtropfen lassen und in eine gefettete Auflaufform geben.
- Zwiebeln fein hacken und in zerlassener Butter dünsten. Lauch und Pilze klein schneiden. Alles zusammen mit Creme fraiche, 2/3 vom Käse, Salz und Pfeffer in die Auflaufform geben. Gut vermischen.
- Den Auflauf mit dem restlichen Käse bestreuen.
- Bei ca. 200° C 30 Min. im Backofen backen, bis der Käse knusprig und goldbraun ist.

Spinach Spaetzle Bake

Level
2
Practice

Personen
4
Serves

Zubereitung
15 mins
Preparation

Inaktive Zeit
30 mins
Inactive Time

Ingredients Spaetzle Dough:
9 oz. Flour
4 Eggs
1 tsp Salt
4 tbsp Finely Chopped Spinach

Ingredients Bake:
5 Brown Mushrooms
5 White Mushrooms
½ Onion
1 Leek
Salt & Finely Ground Pepper
6 oz. Grated Gouda Cheese

Preparation:
- For the Spaetzle Dough mix ingredients and knead with dough hook to a sticky dough (See Basic Recipes).
- Bring salted Water to the boil. In batches press gently the dough through a Spaetzlemaker into the water. Cook shortly (until water froths up), take out, drain well and pour into a buttered casserole.
- Finely chop onions and sauté all in melted butter. Cut leek and mushrooms in small pieces. Pour all in casserole. Add crème fraîche, 2/3 of cheese, salt and pepper. Carefully mix all ingredients.
- Sprinkle the rest of the cheese on top.
- Bake in the oven at 400° F for 30 min. until the cheese has melted and is golden brown.

Saure Linsen & Spätzle

Zutaten:

170 g feine Linsen
1 Liter Wasser
1 halbierte Zwiebel
1 Lorbeerblatt
3 Nelken
250 g Rauchfleisch (ggf. veget. Speckaroma)
1 Gemüse- oder Fleischbrühwürfel
Salz
2 EL Apfelessig
2 EL Mehl
2 EL Butter
2 Knoblauchzehen

Zubereitung:

● Auf die halbe Zwiebel das Lorbeerblatt legen und mit den Nelken feststecken.
● In einen Topf die Linsen, Wasser, gespickte Zwiebel, Knoblauchzehen, Fleischbrühwürfel und das Rauchfleisch geben. Alles kurz aufkochen lassen und gut umrühren. Dann bei niedriger Hitze köcheln lassen, bis die Linsen weich sind (regulär ca. 20-40 Min je nach Linsensorte; im Sicomatic dauert es nur ca. 10-15 min).
● In der Pfanne eine braune Mehlschwitze mit Mehl und Butter fertig stellen. Mehlschwitze in Linsenbrühe einrühren und das ganze nochmals kurz aufkochen.
● Mit Essig und Salz abschmecken.
Das Gericht wird mit Spätzle (siehe Grundrezepte) und warmen Saitenwürstchen serviert.

Level
1
Practice

Personen
4
Serves

Zubereitung
10 mins
Preparation

Inaktive Zeit
30 mins
Inactive Time

Sour Lentils & Spaetzle

Ingredients:

7 oz. Fine Brown Lentils
1 qt Water
½ Onion
1 Bay Leaf
3 Cloves
9 oz. Smoked Bacon (or Veget. Bacon Salt)
1 Vegetable or Beef Broth Cube
Salt
2 tbsp Cider Vinegar
2 tbsp Flour
2 tbsp Butter
2 Cloves of Garlic

Preparation:

● Place the bay leaf on the half onion and pin it with the cloves.
● In a pot pour the lentils together with water, prepared onion, garlic, beef broth cube and bacon. Bring to the boil and stir well. Let simmer over medium heat until lentils are soft (approx. 20-40 mins depending on the lentils used; in the pressure cooker it takes only 10-15 mins).
● Prepare a dark brown roux in a skillet (melt the butter, pour in flour and stir until golden brown). Add roux to lentil sauce and stir continuously to thicken it.
● Season to taste with vinegar and salt.
Serve with Spaetzle Noodles and warmed scalded sausages (e.g. Frankfurt style).

65

Käsespätzle

Zutaten:
2 Zwiebeln
1 Knoblauchzehe
50 g Butter
Salz, Weißer Pfeffer aus der Mühle
200 g Geriebener Emmentaler Käse
150 ml Sahne

Zutaten Spätzle:
250g Weizenmehl
6 Eier
1 TL Salz
Wasser & Butter

Zubereitung:
- Den Spätzlesteig nach Grundrezept herstellen.
- Die Zwiebeln in Ringe schneiden und in der Butter rösten.
- In einer gefetteten Auflaufform die Spätzle mit 3/4 des Käses und 3/4 der Zwiebelringe mischen. Sahne unterheben und mit Salz und Pfeffer würzen.
- Zuletzt die obere Schicht mit restlichem Käse bestreuen.
- Im vorgeheizten Backofen bei 180°C ungefähr 10-15 Min backen, bis der Käse gut geschmolzen ist.
- Vor dem Servieren mit den restlichen Zwiebeln garnieren.

Cheese Noodles

| Level 2 Practice |
| Personen 4 Serves |

Zubereitung 15 mins Preparation

Inaktive Zeit 15 mins Inactive Time

Ingredients:
2 Onions
1 Garlic Clove
2 oz. Butter
Salt & White Freshly Ground Pepper
8 oz. Grated Emmental Style Cheese
5 fl oz. Cream

Ingredients Spaetzle:
2 Cups (9 oz.) White Whole Wheat Flour
6 Eggs
1 tsp Salt
Some Water & Butter

Preparation:
- Prepare Spaetzle according to the Basic Recipes.
- Slice onion into rings and roast in butter until golden brown.
- Butter a casserole, pour in spaetzle, 3/4 of the cheese and 3/4 of the onion rings. Add cream and spices, stir carefully.
- Sprinkle rest of the cheese on top.
- Bake in preheated oven at 350 °F approx. 10-15 mins until the cheese has melted and is golden brown.
- Before serving garnish with rest of onions.

68

Kartoffelstriezel mit Kraut

Potato Striezel with Sauerkraut

Zutaten:

500 g Kartoffeln
ca. 500 g Mehl
2-3 Eier
1 Tasse Milch zum Einarbeiten
2 EL Distelöl
250 ml Sahne
250 ml Vollmilch (keine Fettarme!)
500 g fertig gekochtes Sauerkraut

Zubereitung:

- Kartoffeln waschen und in einen Topf mit wenig Salzwasser geben. Zum Kochen bringen und ca. 20 min. weich kochen. Dann kurz abkühlen lassen und Schale abziehen. Kartoffeln durch eine Presse drücken.
- In einer Rührschüssel die Kartoffeln, Mehl, Eier und etwas Milch zu einem geschmeidigen Teig verkneten. Der Teig darf an den Händen nicht mehr kleben.
- Den Teig in gleiche Stücke teilen und in lange, runde (Ø 1 cm) Nudeln formen (den Teig mit den Handballen auf und ab rollen).
- Striezel dicht in Schlangenlinien in eine mit Öl gefettete Auflaufform legen. Die Sahne und Milch dazugeben, bis alles bedeckt ist.
- Im Backofen bei 190°C ungefähr 40 min backen.
- Das Sauerkraut erhitzen und mit den Striezel servieren.

Level
2
Practice

Personen
4
Serves

Zubereitung
15 mins
Preparation

Inaktive Zeit
60 mins
Inactive Time

Ingredients:

18 oz. Potatoes
approx. 18 oz. Flour
2-3 Eggs
1 Cup of Milk (to be worked in)
2 tbsp Safflower Oil
8 fl oz. Cream
8 fl oz. Whole Milk (no fat reduced milk!)
18 oz. Ready-to-Cook Sauerkraut

• Preparation:

Wash potatoes and put them with less salted water in a pot. Bring to the boil and cook approx. 20 mins. until soft. Allow the potatoes to cool then remove the skins. Press

the potatoes though a press.
Put the pressed potatoes, flour, eggs and some of the milk into a mixing bowl and knead to a smooth dough. Make sure, that

the dough does not stick any more on hands. Divide the dough into equal pieces then form them into long, round (Ø 3/8 inch) noodles (roll the dough up and down between the palms of your hands). Place the striezel in wavy lines into a casserole form greased with oil. Add cream and milk until every-
• thing is covered.
• Bake in the oven for about 40 mins at 375°F. Serve with hot sauerkraut.

Schupfnudeln mit Kraut

Schupfnudeln with Sauerkraut

Zutaten:
500 g festkochende Kartoffeln vom Vortag
500 g Mehl
2 Eier
1 Tasse Milch zum Einarbeiten
250 g Zubereitungsfertiges Sauerkraut
3 EL Butter
200 g Geräucherter Speck
Salz & Pfeffer aus der Mühle

Zubereitung:
- Kartoffeln schälen und durch eine Kartoffelpresse drücken. Mit den Händen die Kartoffeln, Mehl, Eier sowie etwas Salz zu einem geschmeidigen Teig verkneten. Milch nach und nach einarbeiten.
- Den Teig aufteilen und lange Nudeln formen. Mit dem Messer schräg kurze Nudeln abschneiden. Oder mit bemehlten Händen zeppelinförmige Nudeln formen.
- Reichlich Salzwasser zum Kochen bringen. Die Schupfnudeln vorsichtig ins kochende Wasser geben und kochen, bis das Wasser aufschäumt. Die Schupfnudeln abgießen.
- In einer Pfanne die Butter schmelzen und bei mittlerer Hitze portionsweise die Schupfnudeln rundum goldbraun braten.
- Inzwischen den geräucherten Speck in feine Würfel schneiden. In einer Pfanne kurz anbraten, die Schupfnudeln dazugeben und vorsichtig darin schwenken.
- Zum Schluss das Sauerkraut unterheben und erwärmen. Mit Salz und Pfeffer abschmecken.

Level
2
Practice

Personen
4
Serves

Zubereitung
45 mins
Preparation

Inaktive Zeit
0 mins
Inactive Time

Ingredients:
18 oz. Waxy Potatoes (from previous day)
18 oz. Flour
2 Eggs
1 Cup Milk
9 oz. Ready-to-cook Sauerkraut
3 tbsp Butter
8 oz. Smoked Bacon
Salt & Freshly Ground Pepper

Preparation:
- Peel potatoes and press through potato ricer. In a bowl mix with hands potatoes, flour, eggs and some salt and knead to a smooth dough. One at a time work in milk.
- Divide the dough into equal pieces then form them into long noodles. Cut the long strings crosswise into smaler pieces.
- Bring a generous amout of saltwater to the boil. Carefully put the schupfnudeln into the boiling water and cook them until the water begins to froth. Drain the schupfnudeln.
- In a pan melt the butter and bake schupfnudeln thoroughly golden brown.
- Meanwhile, cut the smoked bacon into small cubes. Briefly sear the bacon in a skillet then add the schupfnudeln and cautiously toss the mixture.
- Lastly, fold in the sauerkraut and heat up. Season to taste with salt and pepper.

Gebratene Maultaschen

Stir-Fried Filled Pasta Squares

Zutaten:
12 gekochte Maultaschen (Rezept siehe S. 23)
2 Tomaten
2-3 Eier
100 g frische Champignons
etwas frischer Basilikum, kleingeschnitten
1 kleine Zwiebel
Salz, Pfeffer

Zubereitung:
Die Maultaschen in dickere Streifen schneiden. Die Eier verquirlen. Die Zwiebel in kleine Würfel schneiden. Die Tomaten halbieren, Kerne entfernen und in kleine Stücke schneiden. Champignons in Scheiben schneiden.
In einer Pfanne etwas Butter zerlassen und die Zwiebel darin glasig dünsten. Die Maultaschen zufügen, anbraten und mit Eier übergiessen. Nach kurzem Anbraten die restlichen Zutaten zufügen und mit Salz und Pfeffer würzen.

Level
1
Easy

Personen
4
Serves

Zubereitung
10 mins
Preparation

Inaktive Zeit
0 mins
Inactive Time

Ingredients:
12 cooked Filled Pasta Squares (recipe pg. 23)
2 Tomatoes
2-3 Eggs
4 oz. Fresh White Mushrooms
Some Fresh Basil, chopped
1 Small Onion
Salt, Pepper

Preparation:
Slice Filled Pasta Squares in thick stripes. Whisk eggs until fluffy. Chopp onion finely. Cut tomatoes in halves, remove pips and cut in small pieces. Slice mushrooms finely.
In a skillet melt the butter and sauté onions until translucent. Add pasta square pieces, stir-fry them and add eggs. Stir-fry again and add remaining ingredients. Season to taste with salt and pepper.

Maultaschen mit Spinatfüllung

Zutaten Teig:
Siehe Grundrezept Seite 23

Zutaten Füllung:
200 g frischer Spinat
1 Zwiebel
1 Brötchen vom Vortag
100 ml heiße Milch
50 g Räucherspeck, gewürfelt
200 g Rinderhackfleisch oder Bratwurstbrät
Salz, Pfeffer, Muskatnuss
2 EL frisch gehackte Petersilie und Schnittlauch

Zubereitung:
Den Teig nach dem Grundrezept herstellen.
Für die Füllung das Brötchen klein würfeln und in der Milch einweichen. Nach 10 min. Milch ausdrücken. Den Spinat waschen und die groben Stile entfernen. Kurz in kochendem Salzwasser blanchieren. Abgiessen und mit kaltem Wasser abschrecken. Klein schneiden. Mit den anderen Zutaten in eine Schüssel geben und gut vermischen.
Den ausgewellten Teig in Rechtecke schneiden und etwas von der Füllung darauf geben. Die Teigränder mit Wasser bestreichen und zuklappen. Ränder andrücken. Maultaschen entweder in einer Fleischbrühe oder in Salzwasser 10-15 Minuten köcheln lassen. Herausnehmen. Gebraten oder mit Rinderbrühe servieren.

Spinach-Filled Pasta Squares

Level
3
Challenge

Personen
12
Serves

Zubereitung
35 mins
Preparation

Inaktive Zeit
15 mins
Inactive Time

Ingredients Dough:
See basic recipe on Page 23

Ingredients Filling:
8 oz. Fresh Spinach
1 Onion
1 Stale Bread Roll
3.5 fl oz. Hot Milk
2 oz. Cubed Smoked Bacon
8 oz. Ground Beef or Brat Sausage Meat
Salt, Pepper, Nutmeg
2 tbsp Freshly Chopped Parsley or Chives

Preparation:
Prepare dough according to basic recipe.
For the filling pour milk over cubed bread roll. Squeeze milk out after 10 mins. soaking time.
Wash spinach and remove stems. Blanch spinach in boiling saltwater. Drain and refresh with cold water. Chopp finely. Mix with other ingerdients in bowl.
Roll out dough thinly. Cut out rectangles and place some filling on top. Wet edges with water and fold dough ends together tightly. Let simmer in broth or salted water for about 10-15 mins. Serve stir-fried or in broth.

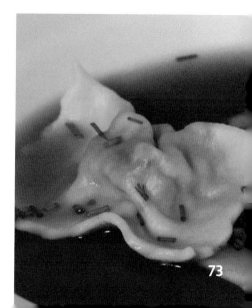

Fleisch
&
Geflügel

Meat
&
Poultry

Hackbraten

Zutaten:
400 g Hackfleisch
1-2 Brötchen vom Vortag
1-2 Hart Gekochte Eier
1 Eigelb
Salz, Pfeffer, Muskat & Petersilie
1-2 Zwiebeln
1 TL Senf
1 Gepresste Knoblauchzehe

Zubereitung:
- Die Brötchen in Würfel schneiden und in Wasser einweichen. Nach ca. 10 min. gut ausdrücken. Die Zwiebeln schälen, in feine Würfel schneiden, in heißem Fett anbraten und abkühlen lassen. Die Petersilie fein hacken.
- In einer Schüssel die eingeweichten Brötchen, Zwiebeln, Knoblauch, Petersilie, Eigelb, Senf, Salz, Pfeffer und Muskat mit dem Hackfleisch vermengen.
- Den Fleischteig zu einer ovalen Form kneten, in der Mitte auseinander ziehen und die geschälten, hart gekochten Eier einlegen. Diese wieder mit dem Fleischteig umschließen.
- Den Strang in eine gefettete Kastenform legen und mit Öl bestreichen. Im Backofen bei ca. 225 °C eine Stunde backen.
- Den Hackbraten entweder noch heiß oder am nächsten Tag gut abgekühlt in dicken Scheiben servieren.

Meatloaf

Level
1
Easy

Personen
4
Serves

Zubereitung
15 mins
Preparation

Inaktive Zeit
60 mins
Inactive Time

Ingredients:
14 oz. Ground Meat
1-2 Stale Bread Rolls
1-2 Hardboiled Eggs
1 Egg Yolk
Salt, Pepper, Nutmeg & Parsley
1-2 Onions
1 tsp Mustard
1 Pressed Garlic Glove

Preparation:
- Cut the bread rolls into cubes and soak in water. After 10 mins. squeeze water out. Peel the onions, cut into fine cubes, roast them in hot grease and allow them to cool. Chop the parsley fine.
- Put the softened bread, the onions, garlic, parsley, egg yolk, mustard, salt, pepper and nutmeg into a bowl; mingle it with the ground meat.
- Form the meat mass into an oval shape then pull it open at the middle and insert the peeled hardboiled eggs inside. Close the meat mass around the eggs.
- Put this mass into a greased baking form and brush on a light coat of oil. Bake in the oven for an hour at about 425 °F.
- Serve the meatloaf hot in thick slices, or well cooled on the next day.

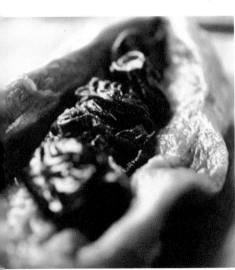

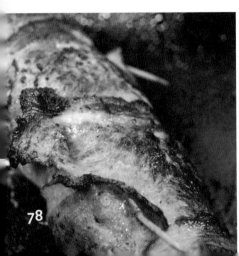

Schweinefilet mit Backpflaumen

Zutaten:
250 ml Weißwein
1 EL Zucker
1/2 Stange Zimt
2 Nelken
150 g Getrocknete Backpflaumen
600 g Schweinefilet
Salz & Pfeffer
8 Scheiben Frühstücksspeck
20 g Pflanzenöl
1/4 L Fleischbrühe
2 EL Creme Fraiche
2 EL Rum

Zubereitung:
- Backpflaumen, Weißwein, Zimtstange und Nelken aufkochen. Vom Herd nehmen und mindestens 1 Std. ziehen lassen. Abgießen und abtropfen lassen, den Weinsud aufbewahren.
- Das Schweinefilet waschen, trocken tupfen und der Länge nach bis zur Mitte einschneiden. Mit Salz und Pfeffer einreiben und mit den abgekühlten Backpflaumen füllen.
- Das Fleisch mit dem Speck umwickeln und mit Garn festbinden. Das Öl erhitzen. Lende darin rundum braun anbraten.
- Die Fleischbrühe und den Weinsud angiessen. Zugedeckt ca. 25 min. schmoren. Fleisch herausnehmen und warm stellen.
- Creme fraiche mit der Schmorflüssigkeit anrühren und aufkochen. Mit Rum, Pfeffer und Salz abschmecken. Das Schweinefilet in Scheiben schneiden und portionsweise anrichten.

Pork Filet with Plums

Level
1
Practice

Personen
4
Serves

Zubereitung
30 mins
Preparation

Inaktive Zeit
85 mins
Inactive Time

Ingredients:
8 fl oz. White Wine
1 tbsp Sugar
1/2 Stick of Cinnamon
2 Cloves
6 oz. Dried Plums
22 oz. Pork Filet
Salt & Pepper
8 Slices of Bacon
1 oz. Vegetable Oil
1/4 qt Broth
2 tbsp Crème Fraîche (lightly soured cream)
2 tbsp Rum

Preparation:
- Bring the mixture of plums, white wine, cinnamon stick and cloves to a boil. Remove from the stove and allow to steep for at least 1 hour. Drain off the liquid allowing solids to drip off; save this wine sauce.
- Wash the pork filet, dab it dry and make a half-deep lengthwise cut. Rub in salt and pepper. Fill the filet with the cooled plums.
- Wrap the meat with the bacon and tie it with thread. Heat the oil. Brown the pork all around in the oil.
- Pour in the broth and the wine sauce. Stew the meat with a lid on the pot for about 25 mins. Remove the meat and keep it warm.
- Mix crème fraîche into the stew liquid and bring it to a boil. Season to taste with rum, pepper and salt. Cut the pork filet into slices and serve in portions.

Fleischküchle

Zutaten:

500 g gemischtes Hackfleisch
1 Ei
1 Bund Kräuter (Petersilie, Schnittlauch)
1 Zwiebel
1 EL Butter
etwas geriebene Zitronenschale
3 Knoblauchzehen
100 g Semmelbrösel
2 TL Senf
Salz, Pfeffer & Paprika edelsüß
2 Spritzer Maggi (oder Sojasoße)
Pflanzenöl zum Braten

Zubereitung:

- Die Zwiebel häuten und sehr fein hacken. In einer Pfanne Butter zerlassen und bei niedriger Hitze die Zwiebelstücke goldbraun schmoren. Abkühlen lassen.
- Das Hackfleisch mit Ei, klein gehackten Kräutern, Zitronenschale, gepressten Knoblauchzehen, Semmelbrösel, den gerösteten Zwiebelstücken, Senf und restlichen Gewürzen in eine Schüssel geben und mit der Hand verkneten. Aus der Masse größere Kugeln formen und flach drücken.
- In einer Pfanne mit heißem Öl die Fleischküchle von allen Seiten anbraten. Die Hitze stark reduzieren und ca. 10 min bei geschlossenem Deckel im eigenen Saft schmoren lassen.

Variante 1: Verwenden Sie Hackfleisch vom Lachs mit Dill als Kräuter

Variante 2: Verwenden Sie Puten-Hackfleisch mit klein gehacktem Schnittlauch

Meatballs

Level **1** Easy	
Personen **4** Serves	
Zubereitung **10** mins Preparation	
Inaktive Zeit **10** mins Inactive Time	

Ingredients:

18 oz. Ground Meat (half Pork & half Beef)
1 Egg
1 Bunch of Herbs (Parsley, Chives)
1 Onion
1 tbsp Butter
Some Grated Lemon Zest
2 Cloves of Garlic
4 oz. Stale Italian Bread, crumbled
2 tsp Dijon Mustard
Salt, Pepper & Paprika Powder
2 Dashes of Maggi-Sauce (or Soy Sauce)
Vegetable Oil for frying

Preparation:

- Peel and finely chop the onion. Melt butter in frying pan, add onion parts and let simmer on low heat until golden brown. Let cool down.
- Mix by hand the ground meat, chopped herbs, lemon zest, finely chopped garlic, bread crumbs, roasted onions, mustard and other spices in a bowl. Form meatballs, your choice of size and flatten them.
- Reheat already used frying pan, add some veg oil and fry meat balls on each side. Then reduce to low heat, cover with lid and let simmer for about 10 mins.

Variation 1: Use ground salmon and chopped dill as herb.

Variation 2: Use ground turkey and chopped chives as herb.

Beef Roulade

Zutaten:

4 Rinderrouladen
100 g Räucherspeck
1 Zwiebel
1 Gelbe Rübe
3 Nelken
1 Lorbeerblatt
125 ml Fleischbrühe
1 EL Tomatenmark
125 ml Trockener Rotwein
Salz
Pfeffer

Zutaten Eier-Füllung:

4 Hart Gekochte Eier
100 g Räucherspeck
4 EL Mittelscharfer Senf
Salz
Pfeffer aus der Mühle

Zutaten Traditionelle Füllung:

4 große Gewürzgurken
100 g Räucherspeck oder Schinken
4 EL Mittelscharfer Senf
Salz
Pfeffer aus der Mühle

Level
3
Challenge

Personen
4
Serves

Zubereitung
30 mins
Preparation

Inaktive Zeit
90 mins
Inactive Time

Ingredients:

4 Slices Beef Braciole(beef very thinly sliced)
4 oz. Smoked Bacon
1 Onion
1 Carrot
3 Cloves
1 Bay Leaf
4 fl oz. Meat Broth
1 tbsp Tomato Paste
4 fl oz. Dry Red Wine
Salt
Pfeffer

Ingredients Egg-Filling:

4 Hardboiled Eggs
4 oz. Smoked Bacon
4 tbsp Medium Hot Mustard
Salt
Freshly Ground Pepper

Ingredients Traditional Filling:

4 Big Gherkins (Pickles)
4 oz. Smoked Bacon or Ham
4 tbsp Medium Hot Mustard
Salt
Freshly Ground Pepper

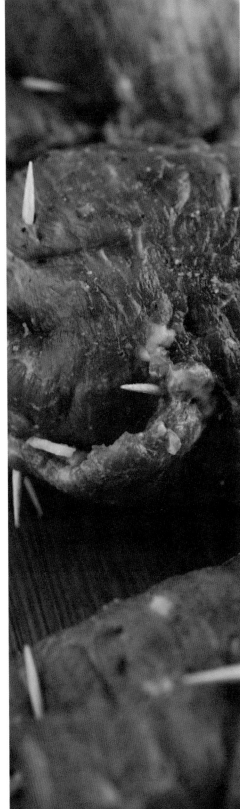

84

Zubereitung:

- Eier hart kochen, abkühlen lassen und schälen.
- Rinderrouladen außen salzen und pfeffern und die Innenseite mit Senf bestreichen. Zuerst mit dem Räucherspeck belegen. Dann entweder jeweils ein Ei oder klein geschnittenen Essiggurken in die Fleischscheiben einwickeln und mit einem Faden festbinden.
- In einem Topf mit erhitztem Fett die Rouladen rundum braun anbraten.
- Die Zwiebel halbieren und auf einer Hälfte das Lorbeerblatt mit den Nelken feststecken. Die andere Hälfte in feine Würfel schneiden. Die gelbe Rübe waschen und ebenfalls in Würfel schneiden. Zwiebeln und gelbe Rüben zu den Rouladen geben und anbraten. Mit Fleischbrühe ablöschen. Die andere Zwiebelhälfte, Wein, Tomatenmark, Salz und Pfeffer hinzugeben und bei geschlossenem Deckel ca. 90 Min. köcheln lassen. Immer wieder umrühren.
- Nach der Garzeit die Rouladen herausnehmen, vom Küchengarn befreien und warm stellen.
- Die Zwiebelhälfte mit Lorbeerblatt und Nelken entfernen. Die Soße durch ein feines Sieb in einen Topf passieren. Mit Salz und Pfeffer nachwürzen.
- Die Rouladen mit Soße auf Tellern anrichten und mit Spätzle sowie frischem Salat servieren.

Preparation:

- Allow the hardboiled eggs to completely cool and then peel them.
- Salt and pepper the beef roulades on their outsides and spread mustard on the insides. Place some of the smoked bacon onto each roulade. Then add small cuts of pickle or one egg on each roulade. Then wrap and tie it closed with a thread.
- Heat some oil and brown the roulades all around.
- Halve the onion. On one half pin the bay leaf with the cloves. Cut the other onion half into fine cubes. Wash the carrot and cut it also into cubes. Add the carrot and onion cubes to the pot with the roulades and roast them. Quench with meat broth. Add the onion half with bay leaf and cloves to the pot as well as the wine, tomato paste, salt and pepper; then cook slowly in a covered pan for about 90 mins.
- After the cooking time, take the roulades out of the pot. Remove the threads and keep roulades warm.
- Remove the onion half with bay leaf and clove. Strain the beef sauce through a fine strainer. Season to taste with salt and pepper.
- Serve on plates along with spaetzle, a fresh salad and the gravy.

Gulasch mit Pilzen

Goulash with Mushrooms

Zutaten:

600 g Kalbsgulasch oder Rinderlende
500 ml Fleischbrühe
2 Zwiebeln
1-2 Knoblauchzehen
Schale von ½ Zitrone
100 g Speckwürfel
2-3 EL edelsüßes Paprikapulver
2 TL Weisweinessig
1-2 EL Tomatenmark
1 Bund Petersilie
Salz, Pfeffer aus der Mühle
200 g Creme Fraiche
2 TL Speisestärke
300 g Pilze (Pfifferlinge, Steinpilze oder braune Champignons)

Level
1
Easy

Personen
4
Serves

Zubereitung
15 mins
Preparation

Inaktive Zeit
90 mins
Inactive Time

Ingredients:

22 oz. Veal Goulash or Beef Tenderloin
17 fl oz. Meat Broth
2 Onions
1-2 Garlic Cloves
Peel from ½ Lemon
4 oz. Bacon Cubes
2-3 tbsp Sweet Paprika Powder
2 tsp White Wine Vinegar
1-2 tbsp Tomato Paste
1 Bunch of Parsley
Salt & Freshly Ground Pepper
8 oz. Crème Fraîche
2 tsp Cornstarch
11 oz. Mushrooms (chanterelle, porcini or brown mushrooms)

Zubereitung:

- Das gewürfelte Fleisch in der Pfanne anbraten, Hitze reduzieren. Speckwürfel mitbraten. Zwiebeln fein hacken und mit dem gepressten Knoblauch zum Fleisch geben. Alles mit Paprikapulver bestäuben und mit Essig ablöschen. Tomatenmark und das Stück Zitronenschale zugeben. Nach und nach die Brühe angießen.
- Gulasch zugedeckt bei mittlerer Hitze ca. 1 ½ Stunden köcheln lassen.
- Pilze waschen, vierteln. In einer Pfanne mit Butter anbraten, mit Salz, Pfeffer, Zitronensaft abschmecken. Petersilie waschen, trocken schütteln und fein hacken, den Champignons unterheben.
- Die Zitronenschale vom Gulasch entfernen. Speisestärke mit 2-3 EL Wasser mischen und unter schnellem Rühren zum Gulasch geben. Die Soße aufkochen, bis sie eingedickt ist. Creme fraiche und Pilze zugeben. Mit Salz und Pfeffer abschmecken.

Beilagen: Reis, Spätzle, Knödel

Preparation:

- Sear the cubed meat in a skillet then reduce heat. Put the bacon cubes in to roast along with the meat. Chop onions finely and add them to the meat along with the pressed garlic. Lightly sprinkle paprika powder over all and quench with vinegar. Add the tomato paste and the piece of lemon peel. Slowly add broth in increments.
- Allow the goulash to cook slowly covered with a lid over moderate heat for about 1 ½ hrs.
- Wash and quarter the mushrooms. Roast in a skillet with butter, season to taste with salt, pepper and lemon juice. Wash the parsley, shake dry and chop it finely then fold it into the mushrooms.
- Remove the lemon peel from the goulash. Mix cornstarch with 2-3 tbsp of water then add it to the goulash while stirring rapidly. Allow the sauce to cook until it becomes thick. Add the crème fraîche and mushrooms. Season to taste with salt and pepper.

Sides: Rice, Spaetzle, Bread Dumplings

Rehbraten

Zutaten Braten:

1 Rehrücken von etwa 1 kg
oder ca. 800 g Schlegel oder Bug vom R
50 g Spickspeck in dünne Scheiben geschnitten
1 Große Zwiebel
2 Gelbe Rüben
Salz & Pfeffer
500 ml Fleischbrühe
1 Glas Rotwein (Halbtrocken)
Bratfett
1 EL Tomatenmark
1 EL Wildgewürz gemahlen
1-2 EL dunkler Soßenbinder oder Stärkemehl

Zutaten Beize:

1 Glas Rotwein
125 ml Essig
600 ml Wasser
1 Zwiebel
Suppengemüse
1 Esslöffel Wildgewürz Gemahlen
1 TL Salz

Das Fleisch muss ganz von der Flüssigkeit bedeckt sein.

| Level 3 Challenge |
| Personen 4 Serves |
| Zubereitung 30 mins Preparation |
| Inaktive Zeit 2 hrs + 1 Tag Inactive Time |

Roast Venison

Ingredients Roast:

1 Saddle of Venison about 35 oz.
or about 28 oz. Venison Haunch or Shoulder
2 oz. Spiking Fat cut in Thin Strips
1 Large Onion
2 Carrots
Salt & Pepper
2 cups Meat Broth
1 Glass of Red Wine (semi-dry)
Butter for Frying
1 tbsp Tomato Paste
1 tbsp Ground Game Seasoning
1-2 tbsp Dark Gravy Thickener or Starch Flour

Ingredients Marinade:

1 Glass Red Wine
4 fl oz. Vinegar
1 Pint Water
1 Onion
Soup Greens
1 tbsp Ground Game Seasoning
1 tsp Salt.
Tip: Make sure the meat is completely covered by the marinade.

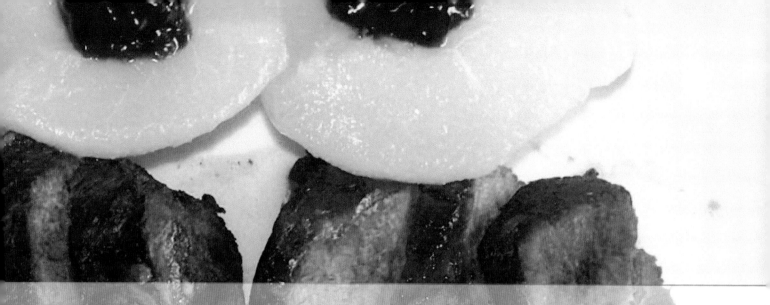

Zubereitung:

Tiefgefrorenes Wild übergießt man nach dem Auftauen mit Wein oder Buttermilch (ca. 12 Stunden). Es muss nicht "gebeizt" werden, weil aufgetautes Fleisch an sich schon mürbe ist. Frisches Wild wird zarter und mürber, wenn es 1-2 Tage in eine "Beize" eingelegt wird.

Fleisch mit Tuch abtrocknen, mit Salz und Pfeffer einreiben. In einem Topf Öl erhitzen. Fleisch mit klein geschnittenen Zwiebeln, gelbe Rüben anbraten. Mit Fleischbrühe und Rotwein ablöschen, Tomatenmark und Wildgewürz zugeben. Die dünnen Spickspeckscheiben über das Fleisch legen, die Soße aufkochen lassen, und anschließend im Backofen zugedeckt bei 180°C ca. 1 1/2 Stunden braten. Falls zuviel Flüssigkeit verdampft, zwischendurch etwas Fleischbrühe nachgießen.

Braten in Scheiben schneiden, Soße durchpassieren und mit in kalter Flüssigkeit angerührtem Stärkemehl binden. Je nach Geschmack etwas süße Sahne zugeben.

- Zum Schluss das aufgeschnittene Fleisch in der fertigen Soße noch ca. 20 Min ziehen lassen.
- Den Rehbraten auf einer Platte mit gedünsteten Birnenhälften und Preiselbeerenmarmelade anrichten.

Beilagen: Spätzle, Klöße und Salate.

Preparation:

- If game is deep-frozen, thaw it. Pour wine or buttermilk over it after thawing then allow it to settle for about 12 hours. It does not need to be "marinated" because thawed meat is already tender. Fresh game will be more tender if it is marinated for 1-2 days.
- Dab the meat dry with a cloth, rub it in with salt and pepper then brown it in a roasting pan on the stovetop along with the onions and carrots (both cut into small pieces). When the browning is finished, deglaze with meat broth and red wine. Add tomato paste and game seasoning. Lay the thin strips of spiking fat over the meat. Heat until the sauce begins to boil then cover it with a lid and put it in the oven for about 1 1/2 hours at a temperature of 350 °F. If too much liquid evaporates, add a bit more meat broth from time to time.
- Cut the roast into slices. Strain the sauce then thicken it, either with a dark gravy thickener or with starch flour that has been mixed in cold liquid. Depending on your taste, add some sour or sweet cream.
- Allow the sliced meat to steep in the finished sauce for about 20 mins.
- Serve roast venison on a large plate, decorated with steamed pear halves and cranberry marmalade.

Side Dishes: Spaetzle, Dumplings and Salads.

Jägerschnitzel

Zutaten:
4 Schweineschnitzel
1 fein gehackte Zwiebel
200 g frische Champignons
2 EL Butter
1 EL Mehl
Salz, Pfeffer, Paprikapulver
125 ml Fleischbrühe
3 EL Weißwein

Zubereitung:
- Die Schweineschnitzel platt drücken, dann mit Salz, Pfeffer und Paprika auf beiden Seiten würzen.
- In der Pfanne etwas Öl erhitzen und die Schnitzel auf beiden Seiten goldbraun braten. Die Schnitzel aus der Pfanne nehmen und in Alufolie warm halten.
- In der verwendeten Pfanne die Zwiebelstücke glasig dünsten. Inzwischen die Pilze in feine Scheiben schneiden und kurz mit den Zwiebeln mitbraten. Mit Wein ablöschen und die Fleischbrühe dazugeben.
- In einer anderen Pfanne die Butter schmelzen und das Mehl einrühren, so dass eine hellbraune Mehlschwitze entsteht.
- Diese dann in die Fleischbrühe mit einem Schneebessen schnell einrühren. Die Soße mit Salz und Pfeffer nochmals abschmecken. Das Fleisch wieder dazugeben.

Dazu passen Semmelknödel, Spätzle oder Schupfnudeln.

Escalope Chasseur

Level
1
Easy

Personen
4
Serves

Zubereitung
30 mins
Preparation

Inaktive Zeit
0 mins
Inactive Time

Ingredients:
4 pork cutlets
1 Finely Chopped Onion
8 oz. Fresh White Mushrooms
2 tbsp Butter
1 tbsp Flour
Salt, Pepper, Paprika Powder
4 fl oz. Bouillon
3 tbsp White Wine

Preparation:
- Flatten the cutlets and season on both sides with salt, pepper and paprika powder.
- In a skillet heat some oil. Sauté the cutlets on both sides until golden brown. Take them out and wrap with tin foil to keep cutlets warm.
- In the same pan and over medium heat braise the onions until translucent. Meanwhile slice thinly the mushrooms and add to onions. Deglaze with white wine. Pour in bouillon.
- In another pan melt the butter. Stir in flour to get a light brown roux.
- Add roux to the bouillon and whisk quickly. Season to taste with salt and pepper. Put cutles into sauce.

Serve e.g. with Bread Dumplings, Spaetzle or Schupfnudeln.

Paniertes Hähnchenschnitzel

Breaded Chicken Escalope

Zutaten:
4 Hähnchenbrustfilets
6 EL Mehl
2 Eier
2 EL Milch
10 EL Semmelbrösel
Salz, Pfeffer, Paprikapulver
1 Zitrone
2 EL frisch gehackte Petersilie
Butterschmalz oder Öl

Zubereitung:
- Die Hähnchenbrustfilets auf beiden Seiten mit Salz, Pfeffer und Paprikapulver würzen.
- Dann mit Mehl bestäuben.
- Auf einem Teller die Eier mit der Milch verquirlen.
- Auf einem anderen Teller die Semmelbrösel ausstreuen.
- Zuerst die bemehlten Filets in der Eiermasse wenden. Dann in den Semmelbröseln wenden. Die Filets müssen gleichmäßig bedeckt sein.
- In einer Pfanne das Öl erhitzen und die Filets beidseitig darin goldbraun anbraten. Die Hitze auf kleinster Stufe zurück schalten.
- Die Pfanne mit einem Deckel schliessen und die Hähnchenschnitzel ca. 5 min. darin aufgehen lassen.
- Vor dem Servieren mit Petersilie bestreuen und das Hähnchenschnitzel mit Zitronenscheiben garnieren.

Beilagen: Kartoffelsalat, Feldsalat

Level
1
Easy

Personen
4
Serves

Zubereitung
20 mins
Preparation

Inaktive Zeit
0 mins
Inactive Time

Ingredients:
4 Chicken Breast Fillets
6 tbsp Flour
2 Eggs
2 tbsp Milk
10 tbsp Bread Crumbs
Salt, Pepper, Paprika Powder
1 Lemon
2 tbsp Freshly Chopped Parsley

Preparation:
- Season chicken breast fillets with salt, pepper and paprika powder on both sides.
- Dust with Flour.
- On a plate whisk eggs together with milk.
- On another plate spread the bread crumbs.
- First dredge fillets in the eggs and then in the bread crumbs. Make sure, that the fillets are evenly coated.
- In a pan heat some oil. Fry chicken breast fillets on both sides until golden brown.
- Reduce heat to low and close the lid. Let steam about 5 mins. to increase size.
- Before serving sprinkle with parsley and put lemon slices on top.

Sides: Swabian Potato Salad, Nut Lettuce

Nürnberger Würste & Kraut

Nuremberg Sausages & Kraut

Zutaten:
8 Nürnberger Würste
3 EL Mehl
1 Dose Sauerkraut
4 Wacholderbeeren
1 TL Butter
Mittelscharfer Senf
4 Brötchen

Zubereitung:
Das Sauerkraut in einen Topf geben und zum Kochen bringen. Die Hitze sogleich reduzieren. Die
Butter und Wacholderbeeren zum Kraut geben
und ca. 10 min. bei niedriger Hitze köcheln lassen.
Vor dem Servieren die Wacholderbeeren entfern-
en oder den Teller damit garnieren.

In einer Pfanne das Öl erhitzen. Die Würste mit
Mehl bestäuben und im heissen Fett rundherum
anbraten. Die Hitze auf die kleinste Stufe reduzieren. Die Würste bei geschlossenem Deckel ca. 5
min. aufgehen lassen.

Auf einem Teller zuerst das Sauerkraut anrichten
und dann die Würste darüber legen. Mit Senf und
Brötchen servieren.

Level
1
Easy

Personen
4
Serves

Zubereitung
10 mins
Preparation

Inaktive Zeit
10 mins
Inactive Time

Ingredients:
8 Nuremberg Sausages
3 tbsp Flour
1 Can Sauerkraut
4 Juniper Berries
1 tsp Butter
Medium-Strength Mustard
4 Bread Rolls

Preparation:
- Bring sauerkraut in apot to the boil. Reduce heat to medium low and add juniper berries and butter. Simmer for about 10 mins.
- Remove juniper berries before serving or garnish the plates with them.
- In a skillet heat some oil. Dust sausages with flour and sauté on all sides. Close skillet with lid and let simmer on low for about 5 mins. The sausages will increase their size.
- On a plate arrange the sauerkraut and top with the sausages. Serve with mustard and bread rolls.

Sauerbraten

Zutaten:
1,5 kg gut abgehangenes Rindfleisch
(Pastorenstück)
Salz, Pfeffer
Trockener Rotwein
Rinderbrühe
1/2 EL Speisestärke oder Bratensoße
50 ml Sahne

Zutaten Beize:
ca. 400 ml Trockener Rotwein
ca. 400 ml Wasser
ca. 100 ml Essig
2-3 Lorbeerblätter
5-8 Wacholderbeeren
6 Pfefferkörner
2 Nelken
1 große Zwiebel
2 Karotten

Zubereitung:
- *Einlegen in der Beize:* Das Fleisch komplett mit Rotwein, Wasser und Essig bedecken. Zwiebel vierteln und Karotten in Scheiben schneiden. Diese zusammen mit den Gewürzen zum Fleisch geben. Bei geschlossenem Deckel im Kühlschrank 5-7 Tage marinieren. Täglich das Fleisch wenden.
- *Braten:* Das Fleisch aus der Beize nehmen, abtrocknen und mit Salz und Pfeffer würzen. Rundherum im heißen Fett anbraten. Die eingelegte Zwiebel und die Karotten aus der Beize schöpfen und mit dem Fleisch kurz anbraten. Mit der Beize ablöschen. Abgedeckt im Backofen bei 200°C ca. 2 Stunden weich schmoren. Oder auf dem Herd bei niedriger Hitze 2-3 Stunden garschmoren.
- *Soße:* Dann den Braten herausnehmen und die Soße durch ein feines Sieb passieren. Etwas Rotwein und Rinderbrühe angießen und kurz aufkochen. Ggf. Soße mit der angerührten Speisestärke binden. Mit Sahne verfeinern und nochmals mit Salz und Pfeffer abschmecken.
Anrichten: Den Braten in Scheiben schneiden und mit Soße servieren.
Beilagen: Spätzle, Knödel, Salat

Sour Marinated Pot Roast

Ingredients:
53 oz. well-hung beef (tri-tip)
Salt, Pepper
Dry Red Wine
Beef Broth
1/2 tbsp Starch or Gravy Powder
2 fl oz. Cream

Ingredients Marinade:
about 14 fl oz. Dry Red Wine
about 14 fl oz. Water
about 3 1/2 fl oz. Vinegar
2-3 Bay Leaves
5-8 Juniper Berries
6 Peppercorns
2 Cloves
1 Big Onion
2 Carrots

Level
3
Challenge

Personen
6
Serves

Zubereitung
30 mins
Preparation

Inaktive Zeit
2 hrs
+ 5-7 Tage/Days
Inactive Time

Preparation:
- *Marinade:* Cover the beef completely with the marinade, made from wine, water and vinegar. Add spices, quatered onions and sliced carrots. Cover pot with lid and put in refrigerator. Let beef marinade for about 5-7 days. Turn beef every day.
- *Roast:* Take beef out of marinade and dab dry with a cloth. Rub it in with salt and pepper then brown it in a roasting pan on the stovetop along with the onion and carrots. Deglaze with marinate. Cover with lid and put in the oven for about 2 hours at 400°F or until beef is soft. Or simmer on low heat on stovetop for about 2-3 hours.
- *Sauce:* Take out beef and strain sauce. Add some wine and beef broth and bring to the boil. Reduce heat and evtl. thicken with gravy or starch flour that has been mixed in cold liquid. Depending on your taste, add some cream and season with salt and pepper.
Serve: Cut beef in slices and serve with sauce.
Sides: Spaetzle, Bread Dumplings, Salad

Herzhaft gefüllte Pfannkuchen

Filled Meat-Pancakes

Zutaten Pfannkuchenteig:

250 g Weizenmehl
2-3 Eier
1 TL Salz
375 ml Milch
Öl zum Ausbacken

Zutaten Hackfleischteig:

125 g Rindfleisch gehackt
125 g Schweinefleisch gehackt
1-2 Eier
1 in Wasser eingeweichtes u. gut ausge-
drücktes Brötchen
Salz, Pfeffer & Muskat
1 Zwiebel und etwas Petersilie, in Fett
Gedünstet

Panade:

1-2 Eier, Paniermehl

Level
2
Practice

Personen
6
Serves

Zubereitung
30 mins
Preparation

Inaktive Zeit
20 mins
Inactive Time

Ingredients Pancake Batter:

2 Cups (9 oz.) Wheat Flour
2-3 Eggs
1 tsp Salt
1 ½ Cups of Milk
Vegetable Oil for frying

Ingredients Filling:

5 oz. Ground Beef Meat
5 oz. Ground Pork Meat
1-2 Eggs
1 Bread Roll (soaked in water then
squeezed out)
Salt, Pepper & Nutmeg
1 Onion, sautéed with parsley in butter

Coating:

1-2 Eggs & Dry Bread Crumbs

Zubereitung:

- In einer Rührschüssel die Zutaten mit der Hälfte der Milch zu einem zähflüssigen, glatten Teig verrühren. Nach und nach mit der restlichen Milch verdünnen.

- In einer Pfanne 1 EL Öl erhitzen und 1 Schöpflöffel Teig einfüllen. Pfanne im Kreis schwenken, so dass ein runder, sehr dünner Fladen entsteht. Wenn die Teigoberfläche fast trocken ist, wenden und kurz backen. Pfannkuchen auf einem Teller abkühlen lassen.

- Für den Hackfleischteig die Zutaten mit den Händen gut vermischen. Anschließend streicht man 2-3 Eßlöffel Hackfleischteig auf jeden Pfannkuchen, wickelt ihn flach zusammen (ca. 2 cm breit) und schneidet ihn in der Mitte auseinander.

- Die gefüllten Pfannkuchen werden paniert, indem man sie erst in zerquirltem Ei und dann in Paniermehl wendet.

- Daran anschließend brät man sie in heißem Fett von beiden Seiten jeweils hellbraun, legt sie schichtweise in eine feuerfeste Form mit Deckel und schiebt diese noch für ca. 20 Minuten in den Backofen bei 100°C, damit der Hackfleischteig ganz durchbrät.

Preparation:

- Basic Dough: Mix the dough ingredients Put flour, cracked eggs, salt and half of the milk into a mixing bowl. Stir dough and add remaining milk gradually to get a semi fluid, smooth consistency.

- In a pan heat up 1 tbsp of oil, put one soup ladle of dough into the pan. Swivel the pan in a circular motion so that a round, very thin, flat pancake develops. When the surface is nearly dry, turn pancake over and briefly bake. Put the pancake on a plate and let cool down slowly.

- Filling: Mingle all ingredients with clean hands. Now spread 2-3 tbsp of the filling on each pancake. Roll up each pancake (3/4" wide - 3/8" thick). Cut in halves or diamond shaped.

- Whisk the egg(s). Dip each filled pancake into the eggs then drain slightly. Next, coat with the breadcrumbs by lightly pressing the crumbs onto the surface.

- When each piece of filled pancake has been prepared, deep-fry in cooking oil until golden brown. Layer them in an ovenproof dish with lid and bake for 20 mins at 225°F, so the ground meat filling is well done.

Zwiebelrostbraten

Zutaten:
4 Scheiben Roastbeef je 150-200 g
oder von der Hochrippe oder Lende
1 EL Öl
1 EL Butter
Salz, Pfeffer
Mehl

Zutaten Soße:
200 g Zwiebeln
2-3 EL Butter
1 TL Tomatenmark
100 ml Weißwein
300 ml Fleischbrühe
Salz, Pfeffer, Majoran
1 TL Aceto Balsamico

Zubereitung:
- Die Zwiebeln in feine Ringe schneiden. In zerlassener Butter glasig dünsten. Das Tomatenmark einrühren und kurz anschwitzen. Mit Weißwein ablöschen und die Rinderbrühe dazugeben. Soße unter gelegentlichem Rühren köcheln lassen, bis sie sämig reduziert ist. Mit Salz und Pfeffer, Majoran und dem Aceto Balsamico würzen.
- Die Soße warm halten.
- Die Fleischscheiben plattieren und mit Salz und Pfeffer würzen. Etwas Mehl darüber streuen.
- In einer Pfanne das Öl erhitzen und das Fleisch darin kurz beidseitig anbraten. Dann die Butter dazugeben und bei geringer Hitze rosa braten. Immer wieder mit dem Bratenfond beschöpfen.
- Fleisch mit der Soße servieren.
  Dazu passen Knödel, Spätzle oder Sauerkraut.

Roast Beef & Onions

Level
1
Easy

Personen
4
Serves

Zubereitung
15 mins
Preparation

Inaktive Zeit
10 mins
Inactive Time

Ingredients:
4 Slices Rumpsteaks (each 6-8 oz.)
or from Prime Rip or Sirloin
1 tbsp Oil
1 tbsp Butter
Salt, Pepper
Flour

Ingredients Sauce:
8 oz. Onions
2-3 tbsp Butter
2-3 tbsp Tomato Paste
3 1/2 fl oz. White Wine
10 fl oz. Beefbouillon
Salt, Pepper, Marjoram
1 tsp Balsamic Vinegar

Preparation:
- Slice Onions finely into rings and cook in melted butter until translucent. Increase temperature to high and stir in the tomato paste. Deglaze with white wine and bouillon. Boil liquid down until smooth consistency. Season to taste with salt, pepper, majoram and vinegar.
- Keep sauce warm.
- Flatten the meat and season with salt and pepper. Dust with flour.
- In a pan heat the oil and roast the meat on both sides shortly. Reduce heat to low, add the butter and cook until center is pink. From time to time drizzle with meat stock.
- Serve meat with sauce.
  It goes well with dumplings, spaetzle or sauerkraut.

Schweinefilet in Paprika-Sahne-Soße

Zutaten:
500 g Schweinelende
2 EL Pflanzenöl
250 ml Sojasoße
1 PK Bratensoße
250 ml Wasser
200 g frische Champignons
1 rote Paprika
1 Zwiebel
250 ml süße Sahne
250 ml Schmand
Pfeffer, Salz, Paprikapulver
125 ml Weißwein oder 7 EL Cognac

Zubereitung:
- Die Lende in Medaillons schneiden und in der Sojasoße ca. 2h einlegen.
- Etwas Öl in der Pfanne erhitzen und das Fleisch beidseitig anbraten. Danach herausnehmen und warm stellen.
- Zwiebel in feine Würfel schneiden. Paprika in feine Streifen schneiden. Champignons in Scheiben schneiden. Im Bratenfond die Zwiebeln, den Paprika und die Champignons ca. 5 Min. zugedeckt dünsten.
- Inzwischen das Wasser erhitzen, das Soßenpulver einrühren und abkühlen lassen. Den Schmand, die Sahne, Gewürze und den Cognac/Weißwein unterrühren. In den Bratenfond mit dem Gemüse einrühren.
- Das Fleisch wieder hin eingeben. Mit der Soße ca. 15 Min zugedeckt köcheln lassen. Ab und zu umrühren. Mit Salz, Pfeffer sowie Paprikapulver abschmecken.

Beilagen: Spätzle, Knödel, Salzkartoffeln

Pork Fillet in Bell Pepper-Cream-Sauce

Level
1
Easy

Personen
4
Serves

Zubereitung
20 mins
Preparation

Inaktive Zeit
15 mins
Inactive Time

Ingredients:
18 oz. Pork Loin
2 tbsp Vegetable Oil
8 fl oz. Soy Sauce
1 package of Powdered Gravy
8 fl oz. Water
8 oz. Fresh Mushrooms
1 red Bell Pepper
1 Onion
8 fl oz. Sweet Cream
8 fl oz. Sour Cream
Pepper, Salt, Paprika Powder
4 fl oz. White Wine or 7 tbsp Cognac

Preparation:
- Slice the loin into medallions and marinate it in the soy sauce for about 2 hours.
  In a pan heat some oil and sear the meat.
- Then remove the meat and keep it warm.
- Chopp the onion in small cubes. Slice the bell pepper and the mushrooms into fine strips. Preheat pan and sauté the onion, bell pepper and mushrooms in the fond for about 5 minutes with lid closed.
- Meanwhile, heat water, stir in the gravy powder and allow this to cool. Fold in the sour cream, the cream, seasonings and the cognac/white wine. Pour into pan with vegetables and stir.
- Put the meat back into the skillet. Covered with a lid, allow it to cook slowly in the sauce for about 15 minutes. Stir the mixture from time to time. Season to taste with salt, pepper and the paprika powder.

Sides: Spaetzle, Bread Dumplings, Boiled Potatoes

Spargel Wrap

Zutaten:
4 dünne Pfannkuchen
4 dünne Scheiben Gekochter Schinken
1 kg Frischer Weißer oder Grüner Spargel
Salz, Butter & Zucker

Zutaten Hollandaise Soße:
200 g Butter
6 EL Weißwein
4 Eigelb
Salz & Pfeffer aus der Mühle
Zitronensaft
Worcestersoße & Cayennepfeffer
300 g Creme Fraiche

Zubereitung:
- Die Pfannkuchen nach Grundrezept herstellen und warm halten.
- Den weißen Spargel waschen, schälen bzw. grünen Spargel gut reinigen und bündeln. In reichlich Salzwasser (bei weißem Spargel noch etwas Butter und Zucker zufügen) ca. 8-15 Min weich kochen. Mit einer Zange aus dem Wasser nehmen und abtropfen lassen.
- Butter zerlassen und etwas abkühlen lassen. Eigelb und Wein im Wasserbad so lange schlagen, bis die Masse dicklich ist. Schüssel aus dem Wasserbad nehmen und nach und nach die Butter unterrühren. Die Soße mit Salz, Pfeffer, Zitronensaft, Worcestersoße und Cayennepfeffer abschmecken. Kurz vor dem Servieren die Creme fraiche hinzufügen und im Wasserbad warm halten (damit Soße nicht gerinnt).
  Auf einem Teller den Pfannkuchen auslegen.
- Den Schinken darin ausbreiten und ca. 5 Spargel darin einwickeln. Die Hollandaise-Soße hinzugeben.

Wraped Asparagus

Ingredients:
4 German Pancakes
4 Thin Slices of Cooked Ham
35 oz. Fresh White or Green Asparagus
Salt, Butter & Sugar

Ingred. Sauce Hollandaise:
8 oz. Butter
6 tbsp White Wine
4 Egg Yolks
Salt & Freshly Ground Pepper
Lemon Juice
Worcester Sauce & Ground Cayenne Pepper
11 oz. Crème Fraîche

Preparation:
- Prepare german pancakes according to basic recipe. Keep them warm.
- Peel skin off the white asparagus or rinse green asparagus and bundle. Simmer in plenty of saltwater (white asparagus: add some butter and sugar) for about 8-15 mins. until tender. Lift bundles from simmering water with skimmer and let drain.
- Melt the butter and let it cool down a bit. Whisk the egg yolk and wine in a stainless-steel bowl on top of a saucepan of gently simmering water. Whisk to a thick consistence. Remove bowl from simmering water and little-by-little stir in the melted butter. Season to taste with salt, pepper, lemon juice, Worcester sauce and cayenne pepper. Shortly before serving, add crème fraîche and keep warm over simmering water (so the sauce won't separate again).
- Put a pancake on a dinner plate, add a slice of ham and about 5 asparagus spears. Roll it up. Pour Sauce Hollandaise on top.

Level
2
Practice

Personen
4
Serves

Zubereitung
30 mins
Preparation

Inaktive Zeit
15 mins
Inactive Time

Kohlrouladen

Zutaten:
1 großen Weißkohl
600 g Hackfleisch vom Rind
1 klein gehackte Zwiebel
1 gepresste Knoblauchzehe
1 Brötchen
1 Ei
750 ml Rinderbrühe
außerdem: Küchengarn

Zutaten Soße:
1/8 L trockener Weißwein
1-2 EL Creme Fraiche
1-2 EL Mehl
Salz, Pfeffer

Cabbage Rolls

Level
2
Practice

Personen
6
Serves

Zubereitung
30 mins
Preparation

Inaktive Zeit
50 mins
Inactive Time

Ingredients:
1 Big White Cabbage
22 oz. Ground Beef
1 Finely Chopped Onion
1 Pressed Garlic Clove
1 Bread Roll (not sweet!)
1 Egg
25 fl oz. Beef Broth
and: Cooking Twine

Ingredients Sauce:
4 fl oz. Dry White Wine
1-2 tbsp Sour Cream
1-2 tbsp Flour
Salt, Pepper

Zubereitung:

- Das Brötchen in kleine Stücke schneiden und in Wasser ca. 10 min. einweichen. Danach herausnehmen und gut ausdrücken.
- In einem Topf Salzwasser zum Kochen bringen. Den Weißkohl waschen und den Strunk keilförmig herausschneiden. Die einzelnen Kohlblätter vorsichtig ablösen. Die dicken Blattrippen der Kohlblätter flach schneiden. Die Blätter in das Wasser geben und ca. 10 min. bei reduzierter Hitze darin garen. Mit einer Schaumkelle aus dem Wasser nehmen und in ein Sieb legen. Kurz mit kaltem Wasser abschrecken.
- Hackfleisch mit dem Ei, Zwiebel, Knoblauch, und Brötchen gut vermischen und mit Salz und Pfeffer würzen. Mit den Händen ovale Klöse formen. Einen Klos jeweils auf ein oder zwei überlappende Kohlblätter geben. Die Blätter über die Fülllung schlagen und die kleinen Päckchen mit Küchengarn festbinden.
- In einer hohen Pfanne etwas Öl erhitzen und die Kohlrouladen rundum braun anbraten. Mit der Rinderbrühe ablöschen. Das ganze bei niedriger Hitze und geschlossenem Deckel ca. 40 min, köcheln lassen.
- Danach die Rouladen herausnehmen und warm halten. Den Fond aufkochen und mit Weißwein ablöschen. Etwas einköcheln lassen und mit in Wasser angerührtem Mehl binden. Creme Fraiche dazu geben. Mit Salz und Pfeffer abschmecken. Soße mit Kohlrouladen servieren.

Beilagen: Salzkartoffeln, Gebr. Schupfnudeln

Preparation:

- Dice the bread roll into small cubes and let them soak in water for about 10 mins. Then squeeze water out.
- In a pot bring salted water to the boil. Wash cabbage and remove the wedge-shaped stalk. Carefully detach cabbage leaves. Cut thicker parts in order to flatten them. Put cabbage leaves into the boiling water. Reduce heat and let simmer for about 10 mins. Take leaves out with skimmer and place in strainer. Rinse quickly with cold water and drain.
- In a bowl mix ground beef, egg, onion, garlic and bread roll. Season with salt and pepper. Form oval meat balls with your hands. Place one meat ball into one or two overlapping cabbage leaves. Wrapp meat ball with leaves and fix little parcels with cooking twine.
- In a high pan heat some oil. Sauté cabbage rolls on each side until golden brown. Deglaze with beef broth and close lid. Let simmer for about 40 mins.
- Then take cabbage rolls out and keep warm. Heat the fond and deglaze with white wine. Let reduce a bit and thicken sauce with -in some water blended- flour. Add sour cream and season to taste with salt and pepper. Serve cabbage rolls together with sauce.

Side Dishes: Boiled Potatoes, Fried Schupfnudeln

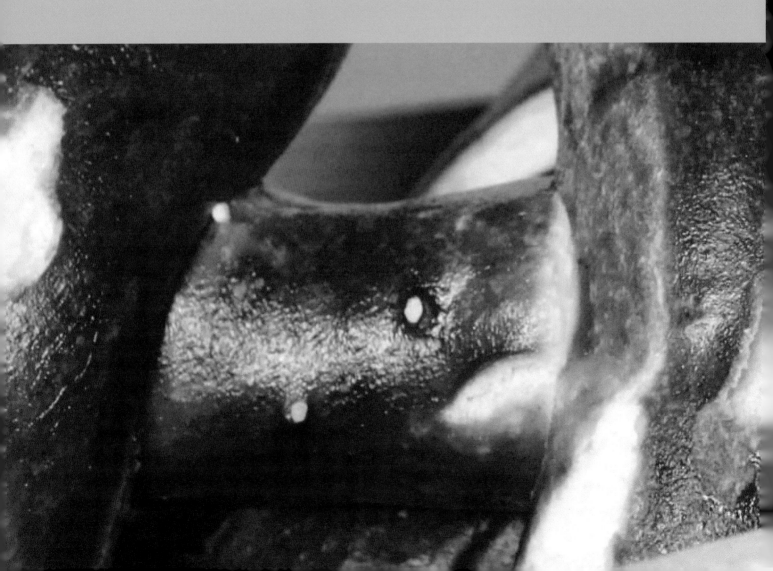

Brot & Pizza Gerichte

Bread & Pizza Dishes

Überbackene Briegel

Zutaten:
300 g Emmentaler Käse
300 g Schinken
1 Zwiebel
1 Bund Schnittlauch
250 ml Süße Sahne
250 g Ungesüßten Joghurt
100 g Weiche Butter

Zutaten Briegelteig:
500 g Mehl (Typ 1050 Dinkelmehl)
2 TL Salz
1 Würfel Hefe
400 ml Wasser
Salz
Kümmel

Zubereitung:
- **Briegelteig:** Mehl mit Salz vermischen. Hefe in Wasser auflösen und mit dem Salz-Mehl verkneten. Den Teig ca. 30 Min gehen lassen. Auf ein mit Backpapier belegtes Backblech ovale, längliche Teigstücke setzen, mit Wasser benetzen und mit Salz und Kümmel bestreuen. Im Backofen bei 220 °C ca. 20-25 Min backen.
- **Überbacken:** Zwiebel, Käse und Schinken in kleine Würfel schneiden. In einer Schüssel mit dem klein gehackten Schnittlauch, Sahne, Joghurt und Butter gut mischen. Den Belag auf die Briegel-Hälften streichen und im vorgeheizten Backofen bei 220 °C ca. 10 Min überbacken, bis der Käse goldbraun geschmolzen ist.

Grill-Baked Briegel-Bread

Ingredients:
11 oz. Emmental Style Cheese
11 oz. Ham
1 Onion
Chives
1 Cup of Sweet Cream
1 Cup of Unsweetened Yoghurt
4 oz. Soft Butter

Level
1
Easy

Personen
4
Serves

Zubereitung
20 mins
Preparation

Inaktive Zeit
65 mins
Inactive Time

Zutaten Briegelteig:
18 oz. Flour (Type 1050 Spelt Flour)
2 tsp Salt
1 Fresh Yeast Cube
14 fl oz. Water
Salt
Caraway Seeds

Preparation:
- **Briegel Dough:** Mix flour with salt. Dissolve yeast cube in water and knead together with the salt/flour mixture. Allow the dough to rise for about 30 mins. Place extended-oval dough pieces onto a baking sheet lined with waxed paper. Brush them with water and sprinkle with salt and caraway. Bake in the oven at 425 °F for about 20-25 mins.
- **Grill-Bake:** Cut onion, cheese and ham into small cubes. Mix these ingredients well in a bowl along with finely chopped chives, cream, yoghurt and butter. Spread coating onto Briegel halves and grill-bake in a preheated oven at 425 °F for about 10 mins until the cheese has melted to a golden brown.

Kauzen mit Speck

Zutaten:

700 g Mehl
250 ml Milch
250 ml Wasser
2 TL Salz
1 TL Puderzucker
1 Würfel Hefe
Fein geschnittener Speck *(alternativ: Käse)*

Zubereitung:

- Das Mehl in die Schüssel sieben, Hefe, Salz und Zucker zufügen und mit dem Teigschaber unter das Mehl ziehen. Die Flüssigkeiten leicht erwärmen und unter den Teig kneten. Zuletzt den klein geschnittenen Speck einkneten.
- Den Teig in der geschlossenen Rührschüssel ca. 1 Stunde gehen lassen.
- Mit dem Esslöffel Häufchen auf ein gefettetes Backblech setzen und bei ca. 220 °C im vorgeheizten Backofen ca. 25 Min backen.

Kauzen Breads with Bacon

Ingredients:

Level
1
Easy

Personen
4
Serves

Zubereitung
10 mins
Preparation

Inaktive Zeit
85 mins
Inactive Time

24 oz. Flour
8 fl oz. Milk
8 fl oz. Water
2 tsp Salt
1 tsp Powdered Sugar
1 Cube of Yeast
Finely Cut Bacon *(Alternative: Cheese)*

Preparation:

- Sieve the flour into a bowl. Add salt and sugar then fold these into the flour with a dough scraper. Slightly warm the liquids and knead them into the dough. Finally knead the finely cut bacon pieces into the dough.
- Allow the dough to rise in a covered mixing bowl for about 1 hour.
- Use a tablespoon to place small globs of dough onto a greased baking sheet. Bake in a preheated oven at about 425 °F for about 25 mins.

Zwiebelkuchen

Zutaten Hefeteig:
1/2 Pkg. Trockenhefe
125 ml Milch
200 g Weizenmehl
80 g Butter
1 Prise Salz
1 Ei

Zutaten Füllung:
1 kg Zwiebeln
3 Knoblauchzehen
200 g gewürfelter Räucherspeck
2 EL Öl
1 EL Mehl
300 g saure Sahne
3 Eier
1 Eigelb
Salz, Pfeffer
1 TL Majoran
1 TL Kümmel
1 MP Muskatnuss

Zubereitung:
● *Teig:* Aus den Zutaten einen Hefeteig erstellen. Diesen in einer Teigschüssel zugedeckt an einem warmen Ort ca. 1 Stunde gehen lassen. Danach rund auswellen und in eine gefettete Springform geben. Einen Rand dabei stehen lassen.
● *Füllung:* Die Zwiebeln und den Knoblauch fein schneiden. Zusammen mit den klein geschnittenen Räucherspeck in einer Pfanne glasig dünsten. Mit Mehl bestäuben.
Die saure Sahne mit Eiern und Gewürzen verquirlen. Die Zwiebel-Speck-Mischung dazugeben und gut verrühren. Pikant abschmecken.
Die Zwiebelmischung in die vorbereitete Form einfüllen.
● *Backen:* Im vorgeheizten Backofen bei 200°C ca. 40 min. backen.

Onion Tart

Level
1
Easy

Personen
6
Serves

Zubereitung
20 mins
Preparation

Inaktive Zeit
100 mins
Inactive Time

Ingredients Yeast Dough:
1/2 Package Yeast
4 fl. oz. Milk
8 oz. Wheat Flour
3 1/2 oz. Butter
1 Dash of Salt
1 Egg

Ingredients Filling:
35 oz. Onions
3 Garlic Cloves
8 oz. Cubed Smoked Bacon
2 tbsp Oil
1 tbsp Flour
11 oz. Sour Cream
3 Eggs
1 Egg Yolk
Salt, Pepper
1 tsp Marjoram
1 tsp Caraway Seeds
1 Pinch of Nutmeg

Preparation:
● *Dough:* In a pastry bowl mix ingredients and knead to a smooth yeast dough. Dust with flour and cover bowl. Allow the dough to rise for about 1 hour at a warm place. Then roll out a circle. Place in buttered springform pan and gently press dough on sides of the pan.
● *Filling:* Finely chopp onions and garlic. Put them together with bacon into a skillet and sauté. Dust with flour.
Whisk eggs, sour cream and filling spices in a bowl. Add onions, galic and bacon and mix well. Seaons to taste. Fill into prepared springfrom pan.
● *Baking:* Bake in preheated oven at 400!C for about 40 mins.

Schwäbischer Salzrahmkuchen

Swabian Salted Cream Cake

Zutaten Salzteig:

500 g Weizenmehl
1 Pkg. frische Hefe
200 g Butter
2 Eier
1 TL Salz
Prise Zucker
250 ml Milch

Zutaten Belag:

1 Bund Schnittlauch
500 g Speckwürfel
4 Frühlingszwiebeln
3 Zwiebeln
600 g Schmand
4 Eigelb
Salz, Pfeffer, Kümmel

Level
1
Easy

Personen
4
Serves

Zubereitung
20 mins
Preparation

Inaktive Zeit
2 hrs
Inactive Time

Ingredients Salty Dough:

18 oz. Wheat Flour
1 Package Fresh Yeast
8 oz. Butter
2 Eggs
1 tsp Salt
A Pinch of Sugar
8 fl oz. Milk

Ingredients Topping:

1 Bunch of Chives
18 oz. Cubed Bacon
4 Green Onions
3 Onions
22 oz. Sour Cream
4 Egg Yolks
Salt, Pepper, Caraway

Zubereitung:

- *Salzteig:* In einer Schüssel Mehl einfüllen und eine Mulde bilden. Darin die Hefe mit lauwarmer Milch und Zucker mischen. Mit Mehl bestäuben. Den Vorteig an einem warmen und zugfreien Ort gehen lasse, bis Mehldecke aufreißt. Dann Eier, Salz und Butter hinzufügen und mit einem Knethaken solange bearbeiten, bis der Teig Blasen wirft und sich leicht von der Schüsselwand löst. Den Teig nochmals ca. 1 Stunde gehen lassen, bis das Volumen deutlich zugenommen hat. Ein Kuchenblech mit hohem Rand fetten und den Teig darin dünn (½ cm hoch) auswellen. Nochmals gehen lassen.

- *Belag:* Schnittlauch, Frühlingszwiebel und Zwiebeln sehr fein schneiden. Zwiebeln in etwas Butter andünsten. Salzkuchen mit Speck, Frühlingszwiebel und den gedünsteten Zwiebeln bestreuen. Je nach Geschmack mit Kümmel würzen.
  Den Schmand in eine Schüssel geben. Die 2 Eigelb, eine Prise Salz und etwas gemahlenen Pfeffer dazugeben und dann alles miteinander vermengen, bis es cremig ist. Auf dem Teig-boden gleichmäßig verteilen, so dass der Boden gut bedeckt ist und der Rand etwa ½ -1 cm frei ist.

- *Backen:* Im vorgeheizten Backofen bei 225 °C ca. 30 Min backen, bis der Rand goldbraun ist. Den Kuchen sofort nach dem Backen in große Stücke schneiden und warm servieren.

Preparation:

- *Salty Dough:* Put flour in a bowl and make a whole. Pour in yeast with lukewarm milk, a pinch of sugar and some of the flour to produce a smooth preliminary dough. Allow it to rise in a warm, draft-less location until flour coating splits open. Then add eggs, salt and butter. Process with a dough hook until the dough develops bubbles and releases easily from the bowl's inside surface. Allow the dough to rise for about another hour. Its increased volume should be readily evident. Grease a cookie sheet with a high rim and roll out the dough thinly (3/16" high). Allow the dough to rise again.

- *Topping:* Very finely cut the chives, green onions and onions. Sauté onions i melted butter. Sprinkle the salt cakes with bacon, green onions and the sautéd onions. Season with caraway as desired.
  Put the sour cream into a bowl. Add the egg yolks, a pinch of salt and some ground pepper then mingle this together until creamy. Spread this evenly on the dough base until it is well covered, up to ¼ inch cm below the cookie sheet's rim.

- *Bake:* Preheat oven to 425 °F. Bake the Cake for about 30 mins until the edges are golden brown. Cut the cake into large pieces right after baking and serve warm.

Süß- &
Mehl-
speisen

Sweet Dishes

Eierhaber (Kaiserschmarren)

Zutaten:

6 große Frische Eier
400 g Mehl
2 EL Puderzucker
2 Prisen Salz
750 ml Milch
Öl

Zubereitung:

- Das Eigelb vom Eiweiß trennen. Das Eiweiß steif schlagen.
- In einer Rührschüssel das Mehl mit dem Zucker, Salz und der Milch zu einem glatten, zähflüssigen Teig verrühren. Das Eigelb unterrühren. Dann den Eischnee vorsichtig unter den Teig heben.
- Das Öl in einer flachen Pfanne erhitzen. Die Hälfte des Teiges in die Pfanne gießen. Langsam stocken lassen. Den entstehenden "Eierhaber" auf beiden Seiten goldbraun braten.
- Dann mit einer Gabel zerreißen. Die Stücke noch etwas brauner werden lassen, dann warm stellen, bis der ganze Teig auf die gleiche Art verarbeitet ist. Je nach Belieben mit Rosinen und/oder reichlich Puderzucker bestreuen.
- Mit hausgemachtem Zwetschgen- oder Apfelkompott servieren (siehe Grundrezepte).

Fluffy Scratched Pancake

Level
1
Easy

Personen
4
Serves

Zubereitung
15 mins
Preparation

Inaktive Zeit
0 mins
Inactive Time

Ingredients:

6 Large Fresh Eggs
16 oz. Wheat Flour
2 tbsp Powdered Sugar
2 Pinch of Salt
26 fl oz. of Milk
Oil

Preparation:

- Separate the egg white from the yolk. Beat the whites until stiff.
  In a mixing bowl mix flour, sugar, salt and milk to a smooth, viscous dough. Mix in the yolks then carefully fold stiff egg-whites into the batter.
- Heat oil in a shallow pan. Pour half of the batter into the pan. Let it set until the surface becomes sticky. Then toss the pancake and bake until golden.
- Tear the pancake apart with two forks. Bake these pieces again until golden brown. Put aside and keep warm. Repeat the process until all batter has been used. If you like, you can add some raisins. Before serving, sprinkle "Eierhaber" generously with powdered sugar.
- Serve with homemade damson compote or apple sauce (see basic recipes).

Ofenschlupfer (Brotauflauf)

Bread Bake

Zutaten:
1 Brötchen
4 Äpfel
6 Erdbeeren
400 ml Milch
50 g Rosinen
3 EL Zucker
1/2 TL Zimt
2 Eier
1 EL Butter
Puderzucker zum Bestäuben

Zubereitung:
- Eine Auflaufform gut mit Butter einfetten.
- Das Brot in Würfel schneiden und in die Auflaufform geben. Die Äpfel schälen und in kleine Stücke schneiden. Die Erdbeeren waschen und vierteln. Äpfel und Erdbeeren in der Auflaufform verteilen.
- In einer Schüssel die Eier, Milch, Zucker und Zimt verquirlen. Gleichmäßig in die Auflaufform eingiessen.
- Im vorgeheizten Backofen bei 200°C ca. 40 min. backen.
- Den Ofenschlupfer mit Rosinen und Puderzucker bestäuen und noch warm servieren. Dazu passt auch Vanillesoße nach Seite 37.

Varianten: Anstatt Erdbeeren können auch Birnen, Aprikosen oder Kirschen verwendet werden.

Level
1
Easy

Personen
4
Serves

Zubereitung
10 mins
Preparation

Inaktive Zeit
40 mins
Inactive Time

Ingredients:
1 Bread Roll
4 Apples
6 Strawberries
14 fl oz. Milk
2 oz. Raisins
3 tbsp Sugar
1/2 tsp Cinnamon
2 Eggs
1 tbsp Butter
Powder Sugar for Dusting

Preparation:
- Grease baking dish with butter.
- Dice the bread roll into small cubes and put in baking dish. Peel and core apples. Cut in small pieces. Wash strawberries, remove stem and quater them. Arrange apples and strawberries on bread.
- In a bowl whisk eggs until fluffy. Add milk, sugar and cinnamon. Evenly pour into baking dish.
- Bake in preheated oven at 400°F for about 40 min.
- Arrange on plates and dust with powder sugar and sprinkle with raisins. It goes well with vanilla sauce on page 37.

Variation: Instead strawberries use pears, apricots or cherries.

Schneckennudeln

Sweet Spiral Yeast Noodles

Zutaten Hefeteig:
500 g Mehl
20 g Frische Hefe
250 ml Milch
140 g Butter
140 g Zucker
1-2 Eier
Eine Prise Salz
Etwas Geriebene Zitronenschale

Zutaten Füllung:
Etwas zerlassene Butter
Zimt & Zucker
Zibeben (Rosinen)

Zum Backen:
1 Tasse Milch mit etwas zerlassener Butter

Level
2
Practice

Personen
6
Serves

Zubereitung
20 mins
Preparation

Inaktive Zeit
70 mins
Inactive Time

Ingredients Yeast Dough:
18 oz. Flour
1 oz. Fresh Yeast
1 Cup of Milk
6 oz. Butter
5 oz. Sugar
1-2 Eggs
A Pinch of Salt
Some Grated Lemon Peel

Ingredients Filling:
Some Melted Butter
Cinnamon & Sugar
Big Raisins

For Baking:
1 Cup Milk with a bit of Melted Butter

Zubereitung:

- *Grundteig:* Alle Zutaten miteinander mischen und zu einem glatten Teig verkneten. An einem zugfreien, warmen Ort den Teig ca. 30 Min gehen lassen.
- *Füllung:* Auf einem bemehlten Backblech wellt man den Teig fingerdick zu einem Rechteck aus. Dieses bestreicht man mit zerlassener Butter, streut Zimt, Zucker und Zibeben darauf und schneidet mit einem Backrädchen ca. 5x3 cm lange Streifen aus. Die Teigstreifen spiralförmig aufwickeln und in eine gefettete Backform setzen. Den Vorgang solange wiederholen, bis der Teig aufgebraucht ist und die Teigspiralen dicht an dicht die Backform auskleiden. Nochmals an einem zugfreien, warmen Ort den Teig ca. 10 Min gehen lassen.
- *Backen:* Eine Tasse Milch mit zerlassener Butter in die Backform gießen und im vorgeheizten Backofen bei 210 °C ca. 30 Min. backen.

Dazu passen sehr gut Apfel- oder Holdermus (siehe Grundrezepte).

Preparation:

- *Basic Dough:* Mix the dough ingredients to a smooth dough and knead it. Allow the dough to rise in a warm, draft-less location for about 30 mins.
- *Filling:* Roll out a finger-thick rectangle on a floured baking sheet. Brush on melted butter then sprinkle cinnamon, sugar and raisins onto the dough. Cut dough in rectangular strips (2"x1 3/16") with a cutting wheel. Roll up both dough halves into spirals and place on a greased baking form. Repeat this procedure until the dough is used up, placing the rolls closely together on the baking form. Allow the dough to rise again in a warm, draft-less location for about 10 mins.
- *Baking:* Pour a cup of milk with melted butter into the baking form and bake in a preheated oven at 425 °F for about 30 mins.

These yeast noodles will be very tender and moist. Serve with apple or elder sauce (see basic recipes).

Dampfnudeln

Zutaten Hefeteig:
500 g Mehl
200 ml Milch
20 g frische Hefe
50 g Zucker
50 g weiche Butter
Etwas geriebene Schale einer Zitrone
1 Ei & 1 Eigelb
1 Prise Salz

Zutaten Flüssigkeit:
50 g Butter
2 EL Zucker
200 ml Milch

& Vanille Soße nach Seite 37

Yeast Dumplings

Level
1
Easy

Personen
4
Serves

Zubereitung
30 mins
Preparation

Inaktive Zeit
2.5 hrs
Inactive Time

Ingredients Yeast Dough:

Dough for about 10 Yeast Dumplings:
18 oz. of Flour
7 fl oz. of Milk
1 oz. Fresh Baking Yeast
2 oz. Sugar
2 oz. Soft Butter
Some Grated Lemon Peel
1 Egg & 1 Egg yolk
Pinch of Salt

Ingredients Liquid:
2 oz. Butter
2 tbsp Sugar
7 fl. oz. of Milk

& Vanilla Sauce on page 37

Zubereitung:

- Mehl in eine Schüssel sieben und eine Mulde formen. Darin die zerbröckelte Hefe mit etwas Zucker und der lauwarmen Milch geben und mit Mehl bestäuben. An einen zugfreien, warmen Ort stellen und den Vorteig ca. 30 min gehen lassen.
- Die restlichen Zutaten hinzufügen und alles mit einem Knethaken zu einem Teig verkneten, bis er Blasen wirft und sich leicht von der Schüsselwand löst. Erneut zugedeckt 1 Std. gehen lassen, bis sich das Volumen verdoppelt hat.
- Dann mit leicht geölten Händen den Teig nochmals durchkneten. Ca. 10 Kugeln formen und auf einem Backbrett dicht nebeneinander setzen. Nochmals etwa 30 Min gehen lassen.
- In einer Auflaufform die Butter zerlassen, den Zucker und die Milch hinzugeben und alles aufkochen. Die Dampfnudeln in die heiße Flüssigkeit setzen und zugedeckt im Backofen bei 180 °C ca. 30 min. backen.

Dampfnudeln passen gut zu warmer Vanillesoße.

Preparation:

- Sieve the flour into a bowl and form a depression. Put crumbled yeast, a bit of sugar and the lukewarm milk into the depression then mix it and dust it with flour. Allow the yeast sponge to rise in a warm, draft-less location for about 30 mins.
- Add the remaining ingredients then knead it all with a dough hook until the dough develops bubbles and releases easily from the bowl's inside surface. Cover again and allow it to rise for about 1 hour, until it has doubled its volume.
- Now, with a bit of oil rubbed onto your hands, knead the dough again. Form about 10 balls of dough and place them close together on a baking sheet. Allow them to rise for about 30 mins.
- Melt the butter in a casserole dish, add the sugar and the milk then bring this mixture to a boil. Put the yeast dumplings in the hot liquid, cover the casserole with a lid then put it in the oven to bake at 350 °F for about 30 mins.

Yeast Dumplings go nicely with warm vanilla sauce.

Aprikosenknödel

Zutaten:

12 gut abgetropfte
Aprikosen aus der Dose
Zimt & Zucker

& Vanille Soße nach Seite 37

Zutaten Hefeteig:

500 g Mehl
200 ml Milch
20 g Frische Hefe
50 g Zucker
80 g Weiche Butter
etwas geriebene Schale einer Zitrone
2 Eier
1 Prise Salz

Apricot Dumplings

Level
1
Easy

Personen
4
Serves

Zubereitung
30 mins
Preparation

Inaktive Zeit
100 mins
Inactive Time

Ingredients:

12 Well Drained Canned Apricots
Cinnamon & Sugar

& Vanilla Sauce on page 37

IngredientsYeast Dough:

8 oz. Flour
7 fl oz. Milk
1 oz. Fresh Baking Yeast
2 oz. Sugar
3 oz. Soft Butter
Some Grated Lemon Peel
2 Eggs
1 Pinch of Salt

Zubereitung:

- Mehl in eine Schüssel sieben und eine Mulde formen. Darin die zerbröckelte Hefe mit etwas Zucker und der lauwarmen Milch geben. Den Vorteig an einen zugfreien, warmen Ort stellen und ca. 30 Min gehen lassen.
- Die restlichen Zutaten hinzufügen und alles mit einem Knethaken zu einem Teig verkneten, bis er Blasen wirft und sich leicht von der Schüsselwand löst. Erneut zugedeckt ca. 60 Min gehen lassen, bis sich das Volumen verdoppelt hat.
- Den Teig in gleichmäßig große Stücke schneiden und runde Fladen formen. In die Mitte jeweils eine Aprikosenhälfte legen. Den Teig über die Aprikosen schlagen und einen Knödel formen. Kurz gehen lassen.
- In einem Topf Wasser zum Kochen bringen. Hitze reduzieren, einige Aprikosenknödel hinein geben und ca. 10-12 Minuten bei geschlossenem Deckel kochen, bis das Volumen sich deutlich vergrößert hat.
- Fertige Aprikosenknödel aus dem Wasser nehmen und abtropfen lassen. Vanillesoße herstellen und in Teller verteilen. Einen Aprikosenknödel darauf geben und in der Mitte aufreißen.
- Mit Zimt und Zucker bestreuen.

Preparation:

- Sieve the flour into a bowl and form a depression. Put crumbled yeast, a bit of sugar and the lukewarm milk into the depression then mix. Allow the yeast sponge to rise in a warm, draft-less location for about 30
- mins. Add the remaining dough ingredients then knead it all with a dough hook until the dough develops bubbles and releases easily from the bowl's inside surface. Cover again and allow to rise for about 60 mins, until it has doubled its volume.
- Cut the dough into equal sized pieces and form round flat cakes. Place an apricot half in the middle of each. Fold the dough over the apricots to form a dumpling. Let the dough rise briefly.
- Bring a pot of water to the boil. Reduce heat, put several apricot dumplings in the water and cook them for 10-12 mins with closed lit until their volume has increased significantly.
- Remove the apricot dumplings from the water and allow them to drip off. Prepare the vanilla sauce and apportion to plates. Put one apricot dumpling on each plate and tear it open in the middle.
- Sprinkle with sugar and cinnamon.

Biskuitwaffeln

Zutaten:
5 Eier
5 EL heißes Wasser
100 g Zucker
Geriebene Schale einer Zitrone
½ TL Backpulver
150 g Mehl
Außerdem: Waffelautomat

Zubereitung:
- Eier trennen und zuerst das Eiweiß zu steifem Schnee schlagen.
- In einer anderen Schüssel das Eigelb mit dem Wasser, Zucker und der Zitronenschale schaumig rühren. Mehl sieben und zusammen mit dem Backpulver unterrühren. Das geschlagene Eiweiß vorsichtig mit dem Schneebesen unterheben.
- Den Waffelautomat aufheizen und die Backflächen mit Öl einpinseln. Einen großen Schöpflöffel Teig auf die untere Backfläche geben und Deckel schließen. Nach beenden des Backvorgangs die Waffeln entfernen und auf eine Servierplatte legen.
- Mit Puderzucker bestreuen.

Dazu passt auch Zwetschgen- oder Apfelkompott, Schokoladensoße oder Kirschengelee.

Biscuit Waffles

Level
1
Easy

Personen
4
Serves

Zubereitung
15 mins
Preparation

Inaktive Zeit
0 mins
Inactive Time

Ingredients:
5 Eggs
5 tbsp Hot Water
4 oz. Sugar
Grated Peel of one Lemon
½ tsp Baking Powder
6 oz. Flour
Also Needed: Waffle Iron

Preparation:
- First separate yolks and whites of the eggs, then beat the egg whites to a stiff consistency.
- Put the egg yolks, water, sugar and lemon peel into another bowl and beat until frothy. Sieve the flour into this mixture, add the baking powder and whisk this in until consistent. Slowly add the whipped egg whites and fold them in with a whisk.
- Heat up the waffle iron and brush oil onto its baking surfaces. Place a large ladle full of dough onto the bottom baking surface and close the lid. When the baking process is finished, remove the waffles and place on a serving plate.
- Sprinkle with powdered sugar.

Waffles go well together with apple sauce, chocolate sauce or cherry jelly.

Schwarzwaldbecher

Zutaten Strudelteig:

500 g Quark
100 g Zucker
1 EL Vanillezucker
100 g Geriebene Zartbitter Schokolade
150 ml frische Schlagsahne
400 g entsteinte Sauerkirschen (ggf. vom Rumtopf)

Zubereitung:

- Den Quark mit Zucker und Vanillezucker schaumig rühren.
- Die Sahne steif schlagen.
- In Dessert-Schalen abwechselnd die Quarkmasse, die Kirschen und die Schokolade einschichten.
- Im Kühlschrank ca. 30 min. kaltstellen.
- Vor dem Servieren mit der steif geschlagenen Schlagsahne und geraspelter Schokolade garnieren.

Tipp: Für ein Kirschengelee ca. 400 g Sauerkirschen aus dem Glas verwenden. 3 EL Kirschsaft mit 10 g Speisestärke anrühren. Den restlichen Saft im Topf zum Kochen bringen und mit der angerührten Speisestärke binden. Hitze reduzieren. 20 g Zucker, 1 P. Vanillezucker und 1 EL Kirschwasser (Obstbrand) einrühren und die Kirschen dazugeben. Zuerst das abgekühlte Gelee dann Schokolade und zuletzt die Quarkmasse in Dessert-Gläser füllen und im Kühlschrank 30 min. kalt stellen.

Level
1
Easy

Personen
4
Serves

Zubereitung
10 mins
Preparation

Inaktive Zeit
30 mins
Inactive Time

Black Forest Cup

Ingredients:

18 oz. Quark
4 oz. Sugar
1 tbsp of Vanilla Sugar
4 oz. Grated Bittersweet Chocolate
5 fl. oz. Heavy Whipping Cream
14 oz. Pitted Sour Cherries (evtl. from Rum Pot)

Preparation:

- Mix quark, sugar and vanilla sugar to a smooth consistency.
- Whip the cream until stiff.
- Fill some cherries in a vitreous dessert cup and top with the quark mixture.
- Keep dessert cold in refrigerator for 30 mins.
- Before serving, finish with whipped cream and grated chocolate.

Tip: For a cherry jelly use 14oz. preserved and pitted sour cherries. Stir 3 tbsp of cherry juice together with 1/3oz. cornstarch. Bring the rest of the juice to boil in a pan and thicken it with the cornstarch mixture. Reduce heat. Stir in 1oz. sugar, 1 P. vanilla sugar and 1tbsp cherry brandy then add the cherries. Let cool down. Fill cherry jelly in dessert cups and top with grated chocolate and quark mixture. Keep cold in refrigerator for 30 mins.

Bratapfel mit Vanillesoße

Zutaten:
4 Äpfel
Saft von 1 Zitrone
100 g Marzipan-Rohmasse
3 EL Mandelblättchen
2 EL Rum
1 EL Calvados
Etwas Butter für die Form

& Vanillesoße nach Seite 37

Zubereitung:
- Backofen auf 180 °C vorheizen.
- Äpfel waschen und mit einem Kugelausstecher das Kerngehäuse entfernen. Innenflächen mit Zitronensaft beträufeln.
- Mandelblättchen in die Pfanne ohne Fett bei mittlerer Hitze hellbraun rösten und abkühlen lassen. In einer Schüssel mit Marzipan, Rum und Calvados gut verkneten. Die Masse in die ausgehöhlten Äpfel füllen. Die gefüllten Äpfel in eine gefettete Auflaufform setzen und im Backofen ca. 25 Min backen.
- Die Vanillesoße zubereiten und mit den heißen Bratäpfeln servieren

Varianten: Anstatt Mandeln können auch Walnüsse, Pistazien oder Haselnüsse verwendet werden; nach Wunsch Rosinen hinzufügen.

Baked Apple with Vanilla Sauce

Level
1
Easy

Personen
4
Serves

Zubereitung
15 mins
Preparation

Inaktive Zeit
25 mins
Inactive Time

Ingredients:
4 Apples
Juice of one Lemon
4 oz. Raw Marzipan Paste
3 tbsp of Shaved Almond
2 tbsp Rum
1 tbsp Calvados
Some Butter to Grease the Form

& Vanilla Sauce on page 37

Preparation:
- Preheat the oven to 350 °F.
- Wash the apples, remove their cores and hollow them a bit with a melon baller. Dribble lemon juice on the inside surfaces.
- Roast the shaved almond in an un-greased skillet at moderate heat until lightly browned then allow this to cool. Knead the marzipan, rum and calvados together in a bowl. Put the filling into the hollowed apples. Place the filled apples onto a greased casserole form and bake in the oven for about 25 mins.
- Prepare the vanilla sauce and serve it together with the hot baked apples.

Variations: Walnuts, pistachios, or hazel nuts can be used instead of almonds; raisins can be added if desired.

Zwetschgen-Pfannkuchen

Zutaten:
100 g Mehl
250 ml Milch
Salz
2 EL Zucker
3 Eier
250 g Frische Zwetschgen (Pflaumen)
3 EL Zucker
1 TL Zimt
Eiscreme (Vanille-, Zimt- oder Milchgeschmack)

Zubereitung:
- Die Eier trennen und das Eiweiß mit 1 EL Zucker und einer Prise Salz, zu steifem Eischnee schlagen und kalt stellen.
- In einer Schüssel das Mehl, Milch, eine Prise Salz und Zucker vermischen und glatt rühren. Das Eigelb unterrühren.
- Zwetschgen waschen, entsteinen und vierteln.
- Den Backofen auf 225° C vorheizen. Das Backblech mit Butter einfetten. Den Teig eingießen und gleichmäßig verteilen. Die Zwetschgen-Viertel auf dem Teig verteilen. Den Eischnee mit einem Esslöffel abstechen und auf dem Teig verteilen. Zimt und Zucker mischen und über den Eierkuchen streuen.
- Das Blech in die 2. Einschubleiste von unten schieben und den Eierkuchen ca. 8-10 Min backen. Den heißen Eierkuchen aufrollen und in Scheiben schneiden.
- Mit Eis servieren.

Level
1
Easy

Personen
4
Serves

Zubereitung
15 mins
Preparation

Inaktive Zeit
10 mins
Inactive Time

Baked Plum-Pancake

Ingredients:
4 oz. Flour
1 cup of Milk
Salt
2 tbsp Sugar
3 Eggs
9 oz. Fresh Damson Plums
3 tbsp Sugar
1 tsp Cinnamon
Ice Cream (Vanilla, Cinnamon or Milk Flavor)

Preparation:
- Separate the eggs. Wisk the egg whites along with 1 tbsp sugar and a pinch of salt to a stiff consistency and put it in the refrigerator.
- Mix the flour and milk, along with a pinch of salt and sugar, to a smooth consistency. Fold in the egg yolk.
- Wash, pit and quarter the plums.
- Preheat the oven to 435 °F. Take the baking sheet and grease it with butter. Pour in the dough and distribute it evenly. Spread out the plum quarters on the dough. Distribute the egg white mass with a tablespoon onto the dough. Mix cinnamon and sugar then sprinkle it over the pancake.
- Put the filled baking sheet onto the 2nd rack position from the bottom and bake the pancake for 8 to 10 mins. Roll up the hot pancake and cut it into slices.
- Serve with ice cream.

137

Apfelstrudel

Zutaten Strudelteig:
300 g Mehl
1 Ei
1 Prise Salz
3 EL Pflanzenöl
ca. 100 ml lauwarmes Wasser

Zutaten Füllung:
2 kg säuerliche Äpfel
75 g Butter
75 g Semmelbrösel
100 g Rosinen
3 EL Rum
Saft von 1/2 Zitrone
5 EL Zucker
1/2 TL Zimtpulver
75 g zerlassene Butter (zum Bestreichen)
Puderzucker zum Bestäuben

Zubereitung:
● **Strudelteig:** Aus den Zutaten einen weichen und glatten Teig herstellen. Er muss sich von den Händen lösen.Eine Kugel formen und mit etwas Butter bestreichen. Mit einem feuchten Tuch abgedeckt ca. 30 min. ruhen lassen. Dann den Teig auf einem mehlbestäubten Tischtuch ausrollen. Mit den Handrücken den Teig anheben und von innen nach aussen dünn ausziehen.
● **Füllung:** Inzwischen die Äpfel schälen, das Kerngehäuse entfernen und in dünne Spalten schneiden. Semmelbrösel in der Butter anrösten. Äpfel, Semmelbrösel und restliche Zutaten miteinander vermischen.
● **Backen:** Die Masse auf dem Teig verteilen und Ränder frei lassen. Den Strudel vorsichtig mit dem Tuch einrollen. Mit zerlassener Butter und ggf. Eigelb bestreichen. Auf ein mit Backpapier ausgelegtes Backblech legen. Im vorgeheizten Backofen bei 180°C ca. 45 min. backen. Zwischendurch mit zerlassener Butter bestreichen. Mit Puderzucker bestäuben. Dazu passt Vanille Eis oder Vanille Soße nach Seite 37.

Variante Quarkstrudel - Füllung: 120 g Butter, 160 g Zucker, 6 Eigelb, 6 Eiweiß (mit 1 MP Salz zu steifem Eischnee schlagen), 500 g Quark (20% Fett), 225 ml Sauerrahm, 60 g Rosinen

Level
3
Challenge

Personen
4
Serves

Zubereitung
30 mins
Preparation

Inaktive Zeit
75 mins
Inactive Time

Apple Strudel

Ingredients Dough:
11 oz. Flour
1 Egg
1 Pinch of Salt
3 tbsp Vegetable Oil
about 3 1/2 fl oz. Warm Water

Ingredients Filling:
70 oz. Apples
3 oz. Butter
3 oz. Bread Crumbs
4 oz. Raisins
3 tbsp Rum
Juice of 1/2 Lemon
5 tbsp Sugar
1/2 tsp Cinnamon Powder
3 oz. Melted Butter (for coating)
Powder Sugar (for dusting)

Preparation:
● **Strudel Dough:** Knead all Ingredients to a smooth dough, that does not stick anymore on your hands. Form a bowl, brush with melted butter and cover with damp kitchen towel. Give it a rest for about 30 mins. Then roll out dough on a with flour dusted kitchen towel. Then lift dough with the back of your hand and pull gently the dough from inside out.
● **Filling:** Peel and core apples. Cut in small slices. Roast the bread crumbs in melted butter. Mix apples, bread crumbs and other ingredients together.
● **Baking:** Spread the filling on the dough evenly. But do not put filling on the edges. Roll dough with kitchen towel and brush edges and outer sides with butter. Eventually brush with egg yolk. Place on a baking sheet with parchment paper. Beke in oven at 360°F for about 45 mins. From time to time brush with melted butter. Al last dust with powder sugar and serve with vanilla ice cream or vanilla sauce on page 37.

Variation Quark Strudel - Filling: 5 oz. Butter, 6 1/2 oz. Zucker, 6 Egg Yolk, 6 Egg Whites (beat with a pinch of salt until stiff), 18 oz. Quark (20% Fat), 7 fl oz. Sour Cream, 2 1/2 oz. Raisins

Kaffee & Kuchen

Coffee & Cake

Zwetschgenkuchen mit Streusel

Zutaten Hefeteig:
500 g Mehl
250 ml lauwarme Milch
100 g Zucker
1 Ei
Eine Prise Salz
100 g Butter
1 Würfel frische Hefe

Zutaten Belag:
1-2 kg Zwetschgen (Pflaumen)
Etwas Zimt

Zutaten Streusel:
200 g Mehl
150 g Butter
150 g Zucker

Zubereitung:
- **Hefeteig:** Mehl in eine Schüssel sieben und eine Mulde formen. Darin die zerbröckelte Hefe mit etwas Zucker und der lauwarmen Milch geben und mit Mehl bestäuben. An einen zugfreien, warmen Ort stellen und den Vorteig ca. 30 min. gehen lassen. Die restlichen Zutaten hinzufügen und alles mit einem Knethaken zu einem Teig verkneten, bis der Teig Blasen wirft und sich leicht von der Schüsselwand löst. Erneut zugedeckt ca. 30 Min gehen lassen.
- **Belag:** Zwetschgen waschen, in der Mitte durchschneiden und Kerne entfernen. Den Hefeteig auf einem gefetteten Backblech ausbreiten. Mit den Zwetschgen schichtweise belegen und mit etwas Zimt bestreuen.
- **Streusel:** In einer Schüssel die Zutaten von Hand miteinander verkneten, bis sich unregelmäßig große Klümpchen gebildet haben. Streusel über den gesamten Kuchen verteilen.
- **Im Backofen** bei 200 °C ca. 20 Min. backen, danach bei 180 °C weitere 10-15 Min. backen.

Level
2
Practice

Personen
8
Serves

Zubereitung
30 mins
Preparation

Inaktive Zeit
90 mins
Inactive Time

Plum Streusel Cake

Ingredients Yeast Dough:
18 oz. Flour
1 Cup of Lukewarm Milk
4 oz. Sugar
1 Egg
A Pinch of Salt
4 oz. Butter
1 Cube of Fresh Yeast

Ingredients Topping:
35-70 oz. Damsons (Plums)
Some Cinnamon

Ingredients Streusel:
8 oz. Flour
6 oz. Butter
6 oz. Sugar

Preparation:
- **Yeast Dough:** Sieve the flour into a bowl and form a depression. For the sponge put crumbled yeast, a bit of sugar and the lukewarm milk into the depression, stir and dust the surface with flour. Allow sponge to rise in a warm, draft-less location for about 30 mins. Add the remaining dough ingredients then knead it all with a dough hook until the dough develops bubbles and releases easily from the bowl's inside surface. Allow the covered dough to rise again for about 30 mins.
- **Topping:** Wash the damsons, cut them through in the middle and remove the pits. Spread out the yeast dough on a greased baking sheet. Top it with a layer of damsons and sprinkle on some cinnamon.
- **Crumble Topping:** Put the ingredients into a bowl and knead them together by hand until irregular large clumps form. Distribute this crumble topping over the entire cake.
- **Bake** in an oven at 400 °F for about 20 mins. then for another 10 to 15 mins. at 350 °F.

143

Versunkener Obstkuchen

Sunken Fruit Cake

Zutaten:
125 g Margarine
125 g Zucker
1 Päckchen Vanillezucker
2 Eier
150 g Mehl
Backpulver
500 g Obst
(z.B. Aprikosen, Äpfel, Kirschen, Pflaumen)
etwas Puderzucker

Zubereitung:
- Alle Zutaten (bis auf das Obst) in einer Schüssel mit einem Rührgerät vermischen. Es soll ein glatter Teig entstehen.
- Eine Springform einfetten und den Teig gleichmäßig einfüllen.
- Frisches Obst waschen, schälen evtl. von Kernen befreien und ggf. in Viertel schneiden. Auf dem Teig verteilen und leicht in die Oberfläche eindrücken.
- Im vorgeheizten Backofen bei 180 °C ca. 25-30 Min. backen.
- Nach dem Abkühlen mit Puderzucker bestäuben.

Sunken Fruit Cake

Level
1
Easy

Personen
8
Serves

Zubereitung
10 mins
Preparation

Inaktive Zeit
30 mins
Inactive Time

Ingredients:
5 oz. Margarine
5 oz. Sugar
1 Package of Vanilla Sugar
2 Eggs
6 oz. Flour
Baking Powder
18 oz. Fruit
(e.g. Apricots, Apples, Cherries, or Plums)
Some Powdered Sugar

Preparation:
- Except for the fruit, put all ingredients into a bowl and mix them with a mixer until dough is completely smooth.
- Grease a spring form and pour in the dough evenly into the form.
- Wash the fresh fruit, peel and remove pits as applicable. Cut larger fruits into quarters. Distribute the fruit pieces onto the dough and press them gently into its surface.
- Bake in a preheated oven at 350 °F for about 25-30 mins.
- After the cake has cooled off, sprinkle it with powdered sugar.

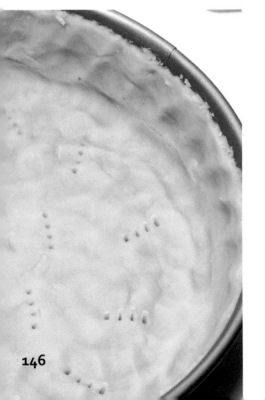

Johannisbeerkuchen

Zutaten Mürbteig:
250 g Mehl
1 TL Backpulver
80 g Zucker
1 Ei
125 g Butter oder Margarine

Zutaten Belag:
4 Eiweiß
220 g Zucker
125 g Gemahlene Haselnüsse
500 g Johannisbeeren

Zubereitung:
- *Mürbteig:* Alle Zutaten zu einem glatten Teig verkneten. In den Kühlschrank für ca. 10 Min stellen. Danach eine Rundform einfetten und mit dem Mürbteig belegen. Dabei einen 3 cm hohen gleichmäßigen Rand bilden. Den Kuchenboden mit der Gabel einstechen.
- *Belag:* Eiweiß mit dem Zucker zu steifem Schnee schlagen. Haselnüsse vorsichtig untermischen und zuletzt Johannisbeeren oder Rhabarber unterheben. Den Belag auf dem Mürbteigboden verteilen.
- Im vorgeheizten Backofen bei 190 °C ca. 40 Min. backen.

Level
1
Easy

Personen
8
Serves

Zubereitung
20 mins
Preparation

Inaktive Zeit
40 mins
Inaktive Time

Ingredients Short Pastry:
9 oz. Flour
1 tsp Baking Powder
3 oz. Sugar
1 Egg
5 oz. Butter or Margarine

Ingredients Garnishment:
4 Egg Whites
8 ½ oz. Sugar
5 oz. Ground Hazelnuts
18 oz. Currants

Preparation:
- *Short Pastry:* Knead all ingredients into a smooth dough. Put in the refrigerator for about 10 mins. Afterwards grease a round form and put the short pastry dough into it. Spread the dough evenly in the bottom and a 3 cm rim around the edges of the form. Puncture this cake base several times with a fork.
- *Garnishment:* Beat the egg whites and sugar to a stiff consistency. Carefully fold in the hazelnuts then lastly the currants or rhubarb. Spread this topping onto the short pastry base.
- Bake in a preheated oven for about 40 mins at 375 °F.

Nußzopf

Zutaten Hefeteig:
500 g Mehl
1 Würfel frische Hefe
125 ml lauwarme Milch
2 Eier
Eine Prise Salz
1-2 TL Zucker
1 P. Vanillezucker
Geriebene Zitronenschale von 1 Zitrone

Zutaten Belag:
150 g gemahlene Haselnüsse oder Mandeln
1 P. Vanillezucker
3 EL Zucker
1 EL Zimt
125 ml lauwarme Milch mit
etwas zerschmolzener Butter

Zum Bestreichen:
1 Ei

Plaited Nut Loaf

Level	Personen	Zubereitung	Inaktive Zeit
1 Easy	**8** Serves	**20** mins Preparation	**90** mins Inactive Time

Ingredients Yeast Dough:
18 oz. flour
1 cube of fresh yeast
4 fl oz. lukewarm milk
2 eggs
a pinch of salt
1-2 tsp sugar
1 Package of Vanilla Sugar
Grated lemon peel from 1 Lemon

Ingredients Topping:
6 oz. Ground Hazelnuts or Almonds
1 Package of Vanilla Sugar
3 tbsp Sugar
1 tbsp Cinnamon
4 fl oz. Lukewarm milk with
some melted butter

For Coating:
1 Egg

Zubereitung:

● **Hefeteig:**
Mehl in eine Schüssel sieben und eine Mulde formen. Darin die zerbröckelte Hefe mit etwas Zucker und der lauwarmen Milch geben und mit Mehl bestäuben. Vorteig an einen zugfreien, warmen Ort stellen und ca. 30 Min. gehen lassen. Die restlichen Zutaten hinzufügen und alles mit einem Knethaken zu einem Teig verkneten. Erneut zugedeckt ca. 30 Min gehen lassen. Danach den Teig in zwei gleiche Teile aufteilen und diese mit einem Wellholz dünn ausrollen (in gleich große Rechtecke).

● **Für den Belag:**
Alle Zutaten mischen und auf die Teigoberflächen streichen. Die Teige aufrollen. Die zwei Teile werden nun in Strickform zusammengerollt und an den Enden zusammengedrückt.

● In eine gefettete Backform geben und mit dem verquirlten Ei bestreichen. Die Oberfläche des Nußzopfes mit einem Messer einschneiden. Im vorgeheizten Backofen bei 175 °C ca. 30 Min. backen.

Preparation:

● **Yeast Dough:**
Sieve the flour into a bowl and form a depression. For the sponge put crumbled yeast, a bit of sugar and the lukewarm milk into the depression. Stir and dust surface with flour. Allow the sponge to rise in a warm, draft-less location for about 30 mins. Add the remaining ingredients and knead it all together by using a dough hook. Allow the covered dough to rise again for about 30 mins. Afterwards, divide the dough into two equal portions and roll each of these out with a rolling pin (into equal-sized rectangles).

● **For the Topping:**
Mix all ingredients and brush it onto the dough surfaces. Roll up the dough portions. These pieces are now to be braided in pairs then pressed together at the ends.

● Put the loafs into a greased baking form and coat them with beaten egg. Cut into the surface of the nut loaf slightly with a knife. Bake in a preheated oven at 350 °F for about 30 mins.

Bienenstich

Zutaten Hefeteig:
500 g Mehl
250 ml lauwarme Milch
100 g Zucker
1 Ei
Eine Prise Salz
100 g Butter
1 Würfel frische Hefe

Zutaten Belag:
100 g Butterfett
150 g geschälte, gehackte Mandeln
150 g Zucker
2 EL Milch

Zutaten Füllung:
1 Pkg. Vanillepuddingpulver
1/2 L Milch
1 Prise Salz
3 Eier
125 g Butter
2 EL Rum

Bee Sting Cake

Level
1
Easy

Personen
8
Serves

Zubereitung
30 mins
Preparation

Inaktive Zeit
85 mins
Inactive Time

Ingredients Yeast Dough:
18 oz. Flour
1 Cup of Lukewarm Milk
4 oz. Sugar
1 Egg
A Pinch of Salt
4 oz. Butter
1 Cube of Fresh Yeast

Ingredients Topping:
4 oz. Clarified Butter
6 oz. Sliced Almonds
6 oz. Sugar
2 tbsp Milk

Ingredients Filling:
1 Package (Set) Custard Powder
17 fl oz. Milk
Dash of Salt
3 Eggs
5 oz. Butter
2 tbsp Rum

Zubereitung:

- *Hefeteig:* Mehl in eine Schüssel sieben und eine Mulde formen. Darin die zerbröckelte Hefe mit etwas Zucker und der lauwarmen Milch geben und mit Mehl bestäuben. An einen zugfreien, warmen Ort stellen und den Vorteig ca. 30 min. gehen lassen. Die restlichen Zutaten hinzufügen und alles mit einem Knethaken zu einem Teig verkneten, bis der Teig Blasen wirft und sich leicht von der Schüsselwand löst. Rund ausrollen und in eine Springform legen. Erneut zugedeckt ca. 30 Min gehen lassen.
- *Belag:* Die Zutaten in einem Topf aufkochen und noch lauwarm auf den Hefeteig streichen.
- *Backen:* Im vorgeheizten Backofen bei 200°C ca. 25 Min backen. Gut abkühlen.
- *Füllung:* Die Eier trennen. Den Eischnee steif schlagen. Puddingpulver, Eigelbe und wenig Milch verrühren. Milch, Zucker und Salz aufkochen und dann das Puddingpulver einrühren. Kurz aufkochen lassen. Den steifen Eischnee unterheben. Butter schaumig rühren und die erkaltete Puddingcreme mit Rum nach und nach zufügen.
- Den abgekühlten Bienenstich in der Mitte durchschneiden und die untere Hälfte mit der Füllung bestreichen. Dann die obere Hälfte drauf setzen.

Preparation:

- *Yeast Dough:* Form a depression. For the sponge put crumbled yeast, a bit of sugar and the lukewarm milk into the depression, stir and dust the surface with flour. Allow sponge to rise in a warm, draft-less location for about 30 mins. Add the remaining dough ingredients then knead it all with a dough hook until the dough develops bubbles and releases easily from the bowl's inside surface. Roll out circle and place in springform pan. Allow the covered dough to rise again for about 30 mins.
- *Topping:* Bring ingredients in a pot to the boil. Spread warm on risen yeast dough.
- *Bake* the cake in preheated oven at 400°F for about 25 mins. Let cool down.
- *Filling:* Separate eggs. Beat the egg white untill stiff. Mix custard powder, egg yolk and some milk. Bring milk, sugar and salt to the boil and stir in custard mixture. Gently fold in beaten egg white. Whisk butter until fluffy. One at a time fold in custard and rum.
- Cut cooled cake in halves. Spread filling on base and close with other cake half.

Apfeltaschen

Apple Turnovers

Zutaten Quarkblätterteig:
250 g Mehl
2 TL Backpulver
250 g Magerquark
250 g Butter oder Margarine

Zutaten Füllung:
250 g Äpfel
25 g Gemahlene Mandeln oder Haselnüsse
50 g Zibeben (Rosinen)
1 EL Zucker
1 EL Rum
Geriebene Schale ½ Zitrone

Zutaten zum Bestreichen:
Eiweiß
Milch
Eigelb

Level
2
Practice

Personen
8
Serves

Zubereitung
20 mins
Preparation

Inaktive Zeit
45 mins
Inactive Time

Ingredients Pastry Dough:
9 oz. Flour
2 tsp Baking Powder
9 oz. Low-Fat Curd
9 oz. Butter or Margarine

Ingredients Filling:
9 oz. Apple
1 oz. Ground Almonds or Hazelnuts
2 oz. Raisins
1 tbsp Sugar
1 tbsp Rum
Grated Peel of half a Lemon

Ingredients Coating:
Egg White
Milk
Egg Yolk

Zubereitung:

- *Quarkblätterteig:* Alle Zutaten miteinander zu einem glatten Teig verkneten. Diesen im Kühlschrank 30 Min kalt stellen. Dann den Teig zu einem Rechteck auswellen, von zwei Seiten her übereinander schlagen und wieder auswellen. Den Vorgang wiederholen. Den Teig dünn ausrollen und Quadrate oder Kreise von 10 cm Durchmesser ausstechen.
- *Füllung:* Die Äpfel schälen, vom Kerngehäuse befreien und in feine Würfel schneiden. Mit etwas Zitronensaft bespritzen, damit sie nicht braun werden. Mit den Nüssen und übrigen Zutaten mischen. Die Hälfte der Teig-Plätzchen am Rand mit Eiweiß bestreichen und in die Mitte die Füllung setzen. Die übrigen Teig-Plätzchen darauf legen und die Ränder leicht aneinanderdrücken.
- *Backen:* Die Apfeltaschen auf ein mit Wasser überspültes Backblech legen und die Oberfläche mit verquirltem Eigelb bestreichen. Im vorgeheizten Backofen bei 225 °C ca. 10-15 Min backen.

Preparation:

- *Curd Puff Pastry Dough:* Knead all ingredients together to a smooth dough. Chill this dough in the refrigerator for 30 mins. Afterwards, roll out the dough into a rectangle, fold inward from both sides and roll it out again. Perform this process again. Roll out the dough thinly then punch out squares or circles with 4 inch sides/diameters.
- *Filling:* Peel the apples, remove the cores and cut into fine cubes. Sprinkle with a bit of lemon juice to keep them from turning brown. Mix in the nuts and other ingredients. Coat half of the dough pieces around the perimeter with egg white and put the filling in the middle. Use the other half of the dough pieces as top covers and press the top/bottom perimeters together gently.
- *Baking:* Place the apple pockets onto a water-rinsed baking sheet and coat the surfaces with whipped egg yolk. Bake in a preheated oven at 425 °F for about 10 to 15 mins.

Donauwellen

Zutaten Marmorkuchen:
250 g Mehl
1 Pkg. Backpulver
250 g Zucker
350 g Butter
7 Eier
2 EL Kakaopulver
3 EL Milch
6 EL Rum
1 (500 g) Glas Sauerkirschen

Zutaten Belag:
800 ml süße Sahne
Sahnesteif
1 EL Puderzucker
1 EL Schokoladenpulver
Schokoladenglasur

Zubereitung:
- **Marmorteig:** Die Butter schaumig rühren. Nach und nach Zucker und Eier unterrühren. Das Mehl sieben und mit dem Backpulver mischen. Portionsweise mit Rum zum Teig geben und gut vermischen.
Den Teig halbieren. In eine Hälfte Kakao und Milch unterrühren. Die andere Hälfte auf ein mit Backpapier ausgelegtes Blech streichen. Dann darauf den dunklen Teig gleichmäßig verteilen. Die abgetropften Sauerkirschen auf der Teigmasse verteilen.
- **Backen:** Im vorgeheizten Backofen bei 180°C ca. 30 min. backen. Vollständig abkühlen lassen.
- **Belag:** Die Sahne steif schlafen. Sahnesteif und Puderzucker unterheben. Die Sahnemasse halbieren. In eine Hälfte das Schokoladenpulver rühren. Den Marmorkuchen zuerst mit der Schokosahne dann mit der hellen Sahnehälfte bestreichen. Mit Schokoladenglasur überziehen. Mit einer Gabel die Wellen in die Glasur ritzen. Im Kühlschrank aufbewahren.

Tipp: Verwenden Sie Kirschen vom selbstgemachten Rumtopf!

Danubian Waves

Level
1
Easy

Personen
12
Serves

Zubereitung
30 mins
Preparation

Inaktive Zeit
30 mins
Inactive Time

Ingredients Marble Cake:
9 oz. Flour
1 Package Baking Powder
9 oz. Sugar
13 oz. Butter
7 Eggs
2 tbsp Cocoa Powder
3 tbsp Milk
6 tbsp Rum
1 Can (14.5 oz.) Sour or Red Tart Cherries

Ingredients Topping:
27 fl oz. Fresh Whipping Cream
Whipping Cream Stiffener
1 tbsp Powder Sugar
1 tbsp Sweet Ground Chocolate & Cocoa
Chocolate Glazing

Preparation:
- **Marble Cake:** Beat butter until fluffy. Gradually add sugar and eggs. Sieve flour and mix with baking powder. Add with rum to the butter mixture and mix well.
Divide the batter into two halves. Add to one the cocoa and milk and stir well. The other half spread on a with parment paper lined baking sheet. Spread the cocoa half on top. Drain the sour cherries and sprinke cherries on dough.
- **Baking:** Bake in preheated oven at 360°F for about 30 mins. Let completely cool down.
- **Topping:** Beat cream until stiff. Add stiffener and powder sugar and mix shortly. Divide into halves. Add to one the ground chocolate powder. Spread white cream first on marble cake then top with chocolate one. At last melt the chocolate glazing and spread on cake. Use a fork to carve waves into the glaze. Keep cool in fridge.

Tip: Use cherries of homemade rum pot!

Käsekuchen mit Streusel

Zutaten Hefeteig:
250 g Mehl
15 g Hefe
125 ml lauwarme Milch
40 g Margarine
1 EL Zucker
1 Prise Salz

Zutaten Belag:
2 Eier
150 g Margarine
125 g Zucker
1 Pkg. Vanillezucker
geriebene Schale und Saft von 1 Zitrone
750 g Magerquark
2 EL Speisestärke

Zutaten Streusel:
125 g zerlassene Butter
200 g Mehl
125 g Zucker
1 TL Zimtpulver

Level
2
Practice

Personen
8
Serves

Zubereitung
20 mins
Preparation

Inaktive Zeit
45 mins
Inactive Time

Cheese Streusel Cake

Ingredients Yeast Dough:
9 oz. Flour
1/2 oz. Yeast
4 fl. oz. Lukewarm Milk
1 1/2 oz. Margarine
1 tbsp Sugar
Dash of Salt

Ingredients Filling:
2 Eggs
6 oz. Margarine
5 oz. Sugar
1 Package Vanilla Sugar
Grated Peel and Juice of 1 Lemon
26 oz. Lowfat Quark (Curd)
2 tbsp Cornstarch

Ingredients Streusel:
5 oz. Melted Butter
8 oz. Flour
5 oz. Sugar
1 tbsp Cinnamon Powder

Zubereitung:

- **Hefeteig:** Mehl in eine Schüssel geben und eine Mulde formen. Darin Milch mit Hefe einfüllen und mit etwas Mehl bestäuben. Zudecken und ca. 30 Min an einem warmen Ort gehen lassen. Margarine, Zucker sowie Salz hinzugeben und zu einem glatten Teig verkneten. Den Teig rechteckig ausrollen und auf ein Kuchenblech geben. An einem warmen Ort (z.B. etwas offener Backofen bei 50°C) nochmals ca. 30 min. gehen lassen.
- **Füllung:** Eier schaumig rühren und Margarine, Zucker und Vanillezucker unterrühren. Zitronenschalen und -saft, Quark und Speisestärke dazugeben und mischen. Die Käsecreme auf den Hefeteig streichen.
- **Streusel:** Butter, Mehl, Zucker und Zimt, mit den Händen vermischen und zu Streuseln verarbeiten. Diese über der Käsemasse verteilen.
- **Backen:** Im vorgeheizten Backofen bei 200°C ca. 35 Min backen.

Preparation:

- **Yeast Dough:** Form a depression. For the sponge put crumbled yeast and the lukewarm milk into the depression, stir and dust the surface with flour. Allow sponge to rise in a warm, draft-less location for about 30 mins. Add the remaining dough ingredients then knead it all with a dough hook until the dough develops bubbles and releases easily from the bowl's inside surface. Roll out a rectangle and place on baking sheet. Allow the dough to rise again for about 30 mins at a warm place (e.g. heat oven to 100°F and place in sheet, and leave door ajar).
- **Filling:** In a bowl beat eggs, margarine, sugar and vanilla sugar until fluffy. Add lemon juice and peel, quark and cornstarch and gently mix in.
- **Streusel:** Mix ingredients with hands to crumbles. Spread evenly over filling.
- **Baking:** Bake in preheated oven at 400°F for about 35 mins.

Apfelkuchen

Zutaten Mürbteig:
250 g Mehl
1 Ei
100 g Zucker
100 g Butter oder Margarine
1 Prise Salz

Zutaten Füllung:
4-5 säuerliche Äpfel
50 g Rosinen
3 EL Rum
geriebene Schale einer Zitrone
1 TL Zimtpulver
4 EL Zucker
3 Eier
2 EL Mehl
200 g süße Sahne
50 g Mandelplättchen

Zubereitung:
- **Mürbteig:** Alle Zutaten zu einem glatten Teig verkneten. In den Kühlschrank für ca. 10 Min stellen. Danach eine Rundform einfetten und mit dem Mürbteig belegen. Dabei einen 3 cm hohen gleichmäßigen Rand bilden. Den Kuchenboden mit der Gabel einstechen.
- **Apfelfüllung:** In einer Schüssel die Rosinen mit Rum, der Zitronenschale, dem Zimt und 1 EL Zucker mischen. Die Äpfel schälen, entkernen und in kleine Stücke schneiden. In die Schüssel dazugeben und alles gut mischen. Dann auf den vorbereiteten Mürbteig verteilen.
- **Sahneguß:** In einer Rührschüssel die Eier und 3 EL Zucker schaumig schlagen. Das Mehl nach und nach dazugeben. Zum Schluß die Sahne unterrühren. Den Guß gleichmäßig über die Apfelmischung gießen.
- **Belag:** Mit den Mandelplättchen bestreuen.
- **Backen:** Im vorgeheizten Backofen bei 225°C ca. 40-50 min. auf der unteren Schiene backen. Nach dem Abkühlen mit Rumsahne servieren.

Apple Cake

Level
1
Easy

Personen
10
Serves

Zubereitung
30 mins
Preparation

Inaktive Zeit
45 mins
Inactive Time

Ingredients Short Pastry:
9 oz. Flour
1 Egg
4 oz. Sugar
4 oz. Butter or Margarine
1 Pinch of Salt

Ingredients Filling:
4-5 Tart Apples
2 oz. Raisins
3 tbsp Rum
Zest of 1 Lemon
1 tsp Cinnamon Powder
4 tbsp Sugar
3 Eggs
2 tbsp Flour
8 oz. Cream
2 oz. Peeled and Sliced Almonds

Preparation:
- **Short Pastry:** Knead all ingredients into a smooth dough. Put in the refrigerator for about 10 mins. Afterwards grease a round form and put the short pastry dough into it. Spread the dough evenly in the bottom and a 3 cm rim around the edges of the form. Puncture cake base several times with fork.
- **Apple Filling:** In a bowl mix raisins, rum, lemon zest, cinnamon and 1 tbsp sugar. Peel apples, remove core and cut apples in small pieces. Toss with other ingredients in bowl and spread on prepared short pastry.
- **Cream Topping:** In a pastry bowl whisk eggs and 3 tbsp sugar until fluffy. One at a time add flour. At last mix in cream. Pour topping evenly on applemixture into the form.
- **Last Topping:** Sprinkle Almonds on top.
- **Baking:** Bake cake in preheated oven at 435°F for about 40-50 mins on lower rack. After cooling serve with whipped rum cream

Biskuit Rolle

Zutaten Biskuitboden:
4 Eier
4 EL kaltes Wasser
200 g Zucker
1 P. Vanillezucker
80 g Mehl
80 g Speisestärke
1 TL Backpulver
etwas Zucker
sauberes Geschirrtuch

Zutaten Füllung:
2 Becher süße Sahne
1-2 P. Sahnesteif
3 EL Puderzucker
2-3 frische Bananen oder 850 g Erdbeeren
bzw. anderes Obst

Zubereitung:
- **Biskuit-Teig:** Eier aufschlagen und Eiweiß vom Eigelb trennen. In einer Rührschüssel das Eiweiß mit dem Wasser steif schlagen. Nach und nach Zucker und Vanillezucker dazugeben. Dann das Eigelb unterziehen. Mehl, Backpulver und Speisestärke mischen, auf die Eiercreme sieben und vorsichtig unterheben. Den Teig auf ein mit Backpapier belegtes Backblech geben.
- **Backen:** Im vorgeheizten Backofen bei 200° C ca. 12-15 Minuten backen. Den Biskuit sofort auf ein mit Zucker bestäubtes Geschirrtuch stürzen und das Backpapier abziehen. Den Biskuit rund aufwickeln und abkühlen lassen.
- **Füllung:** Die frische Sahne steif schlagen. Zur Festigkeit Sahnesteif hinzufügen. Mit Puderzucker süßen. Vorsichtig den erkalteten Biskuit-Teig aufrollen. Die Innenseite mit Sahne bestreichen, die Banane and den Rand legen und einrollen. Die Außenseite garnieren.

Variante runder Erdbeerkuchen:
Den Biskuitteig in eine runde Springform füllen. Nach dem Backen den Boden abkühlen lassen und horizontal halbieren. Die Hälfte mit geschlagener Sahne bestreichen und mit Erdbeeren belegen. Evtl. mit Glasur bestreichen. Die andere Hälfte z.B. einfrieren.

Biscuit Roll

Level 2 Practice

Personen 10 Serves

Zubereitung 30 mins Preparation

Inaktive Zeit 15 mins Inactive Time

Ingredients Biscuit Base:
4 Eggs
4 tbsp Cold Water
8 oz. Sugar
1 Package Vanilla Sugar
3 oz. Flour
3 oz. Cornstarch
1 tsp Baking Powder
Some Sugar
A Clean Dishtowel

Ingredients Filling:
2 cups Whipping Cream
1-2 Packages Whipped Cream Stiffener
3 tbsp Powdered Sugar
2-3 Fresh Bananas or 30 oz. Strawberries or other Fruit

Preparation:
- **Biscuit dough:** Crack the eggs open and separate the whites from yolks. Beat the egg whites and the water in a mixing bowl until stiff. Gradually add sugar and vanilla sugar. Then fold in egg yolks. Mix the flour, baking powder and cornstarch, sieve this mixture over the egg mixture and fold it in gently. Put the dough onto a baking sheet covered with waxed paper.
- **Baking:** Bake in a preheated oven for about 12 to 15 mins. at 400 °F. Upturn the biscuit right away onto a dish towel sprinkled with sugar and remove the waxed paper. Wrap the biscuit in the towel and allow it to cool.
- **Filling:** Whip the fresh cream until stiff. Add cream stiffener for further firmness. Sweeten with powdered sugar. Carefully un-wrap the cooled biscuit dough. Spread cream evenly on the inside. Put bananas on the edge and wrap cake. Garnish outside.

Variation Round Strawberry Cake:
Fill Biscuit Dough into round springform pan. After Baking let cool down. Slice horizontally in the middle. One one half spread whipped cream and garnish with strawberries. Freeze or use other half.

Schwarzwälder Kirschtorte

Zutaten Biskuitboden:

4 Eier
4 EL kaltes Wasser
200 g Zucker
1 P. Vanillezucker
80 g Mehl
80 g Speisestärke
1 TL Backpulver
50 g dunkler, süsser Kakao (z.B. Ghirardelli)

Zutaten Kirsch-Füllung:

1 Glas (650 g) Sauerkirschen, entsteint
4 EL Kirschwasser
2 EL Zucker
4 EL Speisestärke

Zutaten Toppings:

2 Becher süße Sahne
1-2 P. Sahnesteif
3 EL Puderzucker
50 g Blockschokolade
Cocktailkirschen

Level
3
Challenge

Personen
12
Serves

Zubereitung
45 mins
Preparation

Inaktive Zeit
1 hr
15 mins
Inactive Time

Black Forest Cake

Ingredients Biscuit Base:

4 Eggs
4 tbsp Cold Water
8 oz. Sugar
1 Package Vanilla Sugar
3 oz. Flour
3 oz. Cornstarch
1 tsp Baking Powder
2 oz. Sweeet Ground Chocolate and Cocoa
Powder (e.g. Ghirardelli)

Ingredients Cherry-Filling:

1 glass (24 oz.) Sour Cherries, pitted
4 tbsp Cherry Brandy "Kirschwasser"
2 tbsp Sugar
4 tbsp Cornstarch

Ingredients Toppings:

2 cups Whipping Cream
1-2 Packages Whipped Cream Stiffener
3 tbsp Powdered Sugar
2 oz. Non-Sweet Chocolate Bar
Cocktail Cherries

Zubereitung:

- **Biskuit-Teig:** Eier aufschlagen und Eiweiß vom Eigelb trennen. In einer Rührschüssel das Eiweiß mit dem Wasser steif schlagen. Nach und nach Zucker und Vanillezucker dazugeben. Dann das Eigelb unterziehen. Mehl, Speisestärke, Backpulver und Kakao mischen, auf die Eiercreme sieben und vorsichtig unterheben. In ein gefettete Springform oder Muffinförmchen verteilen.
- **Backen:** Im vorgeheizten Backofen bei 200° C ca. 12-15 Minuten backen. Vollständig abkühlen lassen (ca. 1 Stunde) und horizontal halbieren oder dritteln. (Muffins mit Kugelausstecher aushölen).
- **Kirsch-Füllung:** Die Kirschen abtropfen lassen, Saft auffangen. Stärke mit etwas Kirschsaft verrühren. Übrigen Kirschsaft mit Zucker in einem Topf aufkochen. Die Stärke einrühren bis die Masse dicklich wird. Vom Herd nehmen, Kirschwasser und Kirschen unterrühren. Auf dem Biskuitboden verteilen (ggf. in Muffins einfüllen). Den Biskuitdeckel auflegen (Muffins ohne Deckel).
- **Toppings:** Die frische Sahne steif schlagen. Zur Festigkeit Sahnesteif hinzufügen. Mit Puderzucker süßen. Die Kirsch-Biskuittorte mit Sahne bestreichen (Muffins spiralförmig mit Sahne auffüllen).
Blockschokolade auf einem Hobel in eine Richtung schaben, damit blättrige Späne entstehen. Torte damit verzieren.
Zum Schluss die Coctailkirschen auflegen.
Bis zum Servieren kalt stellen.

Preparation:

- **Biscuit dough:** Crack the eggs open and separate the whites from yolks. Beat the egg whites and the water in a mixing bowl until stiff. Gradually add sugar and vanilla sugar. Then fold in egg yolks. Mix the flour, baking powder, cornstarch and cacao, sieve this mixture over the egg mixture and fold it in gently. Put the dough onto a greased springform pan or muffin baking pan.
- **Baking:** Bake in a preheated oven for about 12 to 15 mins. at 400 °F. Allow it to cool down completely (ca. 1 hour). Then slice horizontally in the middle (or slice two times).
- **Cherry-Filling:** Drain Cherries and catch its juice. In a cup mix some juice with starch to a smooth consistency. In a pot bring the cherry juice and sugar to the boil. Add starch and stir frequently until thickened. Put aside and stir in cherries and cherry brandy. Spread across the biscuit base cake. Put other half of cake on top. (Muffins: deepen with melon baller and fill up with cherry-filling.)
- **Toppings:** Whip the fresh cream until stiff. Add cream stiffener for further firmness. Sweeten with powdered sugar. Cover cake with whipped cream. (Decorate muffins with whipped cream by spraying it spiral-shaped).
Slice chocolate bar with staight blade into flakes and garnish the cake with it.
At last garnish with coctail cherries.
Keep cool in refrigerator until serving.

Holidays

Festtage

Alemannian Carnival

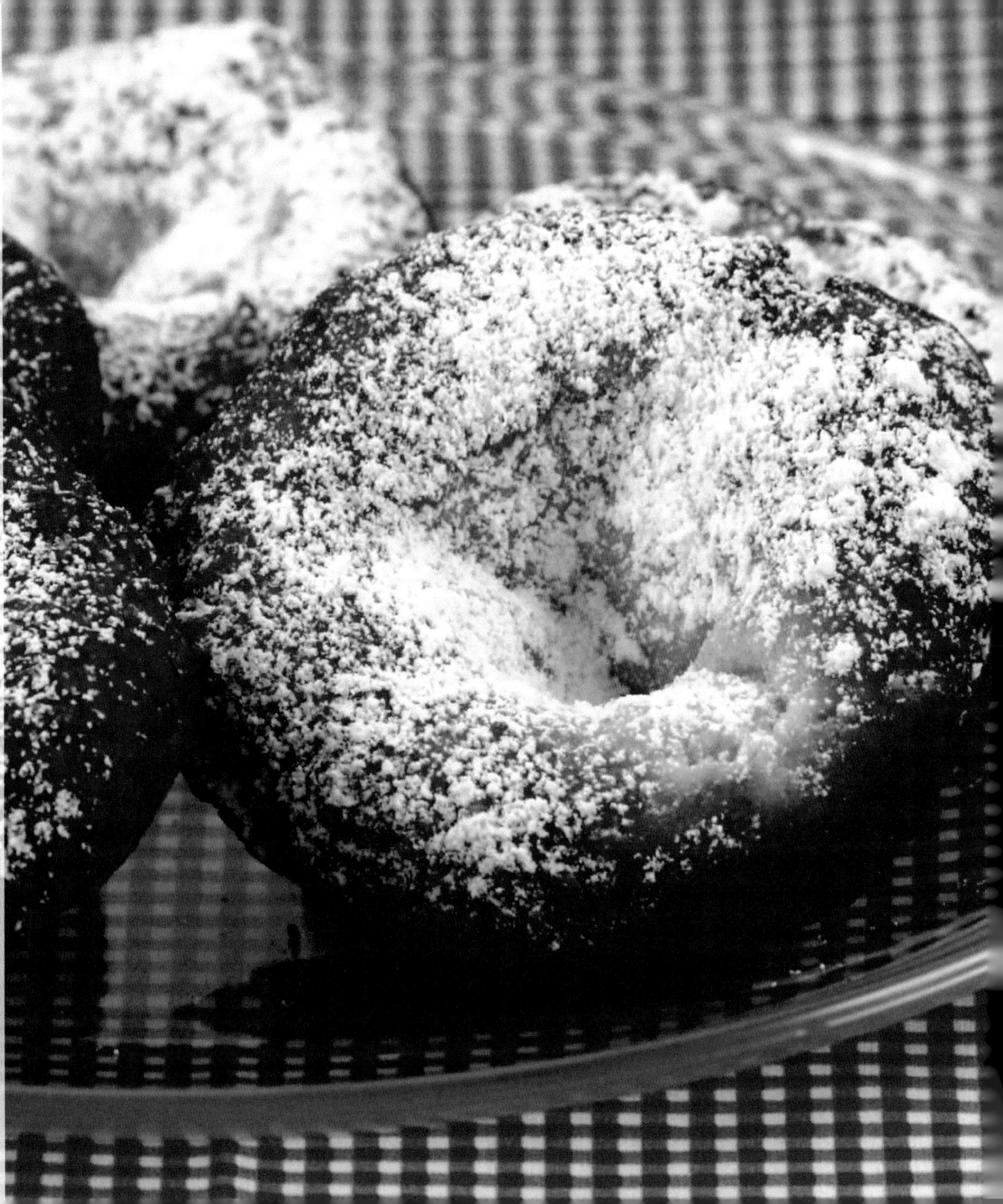

Faschingsküchle

Zutaten:
500 g Mehl
125 g Butter
30 g Hefe
2 EL Zucker
2 Eigelb
Milch
Salz
Schmalz oder Pflanzenfett zum Ausbacken
Zucker zum Bestreuen

Zubereitung:
- Zutaten in eine Schüssel geben und einen festen Hefeteig formen.
- Zugedeckt an einem warmen Ort ca. 1 Stunde gehen lassen.
- Den Hefeteig entweder in kleine runde Kuchen oder in Rauten unterteilen (dazu Teig ausrollen und mit einem Teigroller die Rauten bilden). Auf einer bemehlten Arbeitsfläche nochmals ca. 30 min. gehen lassen.
- Die Teigstücke werden nun mit den Fingern von innen nach aussen gezogen, sodass die Mitte fast durchsichtig wird und der Rand etwas dicker bleibt.
- Die Küchlein werden auf beiden Seiten in heißem Fett gebacken und noch heiß mit Zucker bestreut.

Dazu schmecken Apfel-, Zwetschgen- oder Holundermus (siehe Grundrezepte)!

Carnival Pastries

Level
2
Practice

Personen
6
Serves

Zubereitung
15 mins
Preparation

Inaktive Zeit
30 mins
Inactive Time

Ingredients:
18 oz. Flour
5 oz. Butter
1 Package of Yeast
2 tbsp Sugar
3 Egg Yolk
Milk
Salt
Lard or Vegetable Frying Oil
Sugar for Dusting

Preparation:
- In a pastry bowl knead ingredients to a firm dough.
- Cover bowl and let rise for about 1 hour. Make sure it is a warm and non-drafty place.
- Divide yeast dough into small round cakes or into diamond shaped pieces (for this roll out dough and cut out diamonds with pastry cutter). Put them on a with flour dusted surface and let rise for another 30 mins.
- Take each piece and press gently from inside out, so that the middle appears almost sheer and the edges are thicker.
- Deep-fry carnival pastries on both sides in heated oil until golden brown. Take out and dust with sugar.

Serve with apple-, damson- or elder sauce (see basic recipes)!

Osterlamm

Zutaten:
60 g Butter
60 g Zucker
2 TL Vanillezucker
1 Prise Salz
1 Ei
2 TL Rum
40 g fein gemahlene Nüsse
40 g Dinkelmehl
40 g Speisestärke
1 TL Backpulver
Puderzucker zum Bestäuben
Hasenform zum Backen

Zubereitung:
- Den Backofen auf 180°C vorheizen.
- Die Butter schaumig schlagen und Zucker, Vanillezucker, Salz, Ei und Rum unterrühren. In einer Schüssel die trockenen Zutaten mischen: Nüsse, Mehl, Stärke und Backpulver. Diese dann mit den anderen Zutaten zu einem Rührteig verarbeiten.
- Eine Hasenform mit Butter einfetten und dann mit Mehl oder Gries bestäuben. Den Rührteig einfüllen. Auf ein Backblech stellen.
- Im Backofen auf der unteren Schiene ca. 35 min. backen.
- Aus der Form lösen und abkühlen lassen. Mit Puderzucker bestäuben.

Easter Lamb

Level
1
Easy

Personen
2
Serves

Zubereitung
10 mins
Preparation

Inaktive Zeit
35 mins
Inactive Time

Ingredients:
2 1/2 oz. Butter
2 1/2 oz. Sugar
2 tsp Vanilla Sugar
Pinch of Salt
1 Egg
2 tbsp Rum
1 1/2 oz. Finely Ground Nuts
1 1/2 oz. Flour
1 1/2 oz. Starch Powder
1 tsp Baking Powder
Powder Sugar for Dusting
Rabbit Mold for Baking

Preparation:
- Preheat oven to 350°F.
- Beat butter until fluffy. Gradually add sugar, vanilla sugar, salt, egg and rum.
- In another bowl mix dry ingredients: nuts, flour, starch and baking powder. Add to other ingredients and work them into a batter. Grease the mold with butter and dust with some flour. Fill in the batter and place mold on a baking sheet.
- Bake in oven on lowest rack for about 35 mins.
- Remove from mold and dust rabbit with powder sugar.

Ausstecherle

Zutaten:
500 g Weizenmehl
250 g Butter
200 g Zucker
2 große Eier
1 Eigelb
1 EL Milch
1 Prise Salz
1 P. Vanillezucker
Hagelzucker oder bunte Streusel
Ausstechformen

Zubereitung:
- Die Butter mit 2 Eiern, Zucker, Vanillezucker und Salz schaumig rühren. Das Mehl hinzufügen und die Masse zu einem glatten Teig verkneten.
- Eine Arbeitsfläche mit Mehl bestreuen und den Teig darauf ca. 5 mm hoch gleichmäßig ausrollen.
- Mit den Ausstechformen verschiedene Motive ausstechen und auf ein mit Backpapier belegtes Backblech legen.
- Das Eigelb mit etwas Milch vermischen und damit die Plätzchenoberfläche bestreichen. Mit Hagelzucker oder bunten Zuckerstreusel bestreuen.
- Im vorgeheizten Backofen bei 180°C ca. 12 min. backen.

Variante Schoko-Herzen: Herzförmige Kekse zur Hälfte in Schokoglasur tauchen und auf einem Backpapier trocknen lassen.

Shortbread Cut-Out Cookies

Level
1
Easy

Personen
6
Serves

Zubereitung
20 mins
Preparation

Inaktive Zeit
12 mins
Inactive Time

Ingredients:
18 oz. Wheat Flour
9 oz. Butter
8 oz. Sugar
2 Eggs
1 Egg Yolk
1 tbsp Milk
Pinch of Salt
1 tbsp Vanilla Sugar
Sugar Crystals or Sprinkles
Cookie Cutters

Preparation:
- Whisk 2 eggs, sugar, vanilla sugar and salt until light and fluffy. Incorporate flour and kneat dough to a smooth consistency.
- Roll pastry out on a floured work surface to an thickness of a little less than a quater of an inch (5 mm).
- Cut out different motives with cookie cutter and place them on a baking sheet with parchment paper.
- Mix 1 egg yolk with milk and brush it on the cookies' surface. Sprinkle with sugar crystals or sprinkles.
- Bake in preheated oven at 375°F for about 12 min.

Variation Chocolate Hearts: Cut out hearts and after baking dip one side in heated dipping chocolate. Let dry on parchment paper.

Vanillekipferl

Zutaten:
250 g Weizenmehl
200 g Butter
100 g fein gemahlene Mandeln
150 g Vanillezucker
4 EL Puderzucker

Zubereitung:
Aus dem Mehl, Butter, Mandeln und der Hälfte des Vanillezuckers einen geschmeidigen Teig kneten und diesen ca. 30 min. kalt stellen. Den Teig zu einer Rolle formen und in kleinere Stücke zerteilen. Diese mit den Händen zu Halbmonden rollen und auf ein mit Backpapier ausgelegtes Backblech legen. Bei ca. 175° C ca. 15 min. backen. Puderzucker und restlichen Vanillezucker mischen. Die noch heissen Plätzchen darin wenden.

Vanilla Crescents

Level
1
Easy

Personen
6
Serves

Zubereitung
20 mins
Preparation

Inaktive Zeit
45 mins
Inactive Time

Ingredients:
9 oz. Flour
8 oz. Butter
4 oz. Finely Ground Almonds
6 oz. Vanilla Sugar
4 tbsp Powder Sugar

Preparation:
Knead flour, butter, almonds and half of the vanilla sugar together to form a smooth dough. Chill for about 30 mins. in fridge. Form dough into a roll and cut slices from it. Shape them into small crescents. and place them on a baking sheet with parchment paper. Bake in preheated oven at 350°F for about 15 mins. Mix vanilla and powder sugars. Coat with it crescents while they are still hot.

Kokosmakronen

Zutaten:
100 g Margarine
100 g Zucker
2 P. Vanillezucker
1 TL Vanillearoma
1 Ei
150 g Weizenmehl
75 g Speisestärke
2 TL Backpulver
200 g Kokosraspeln
etwas geriebene Zitronenschale

Zubereitung:
Alle Zutaten in eine Backschüssel geben und einen festen Rührteig herstellen. Mit einem Teelöffel kleine Teighäufchen formen und auf ein mit Backpapier belegtes Backblech setzen. Im vorgeheizten Backofen bei 180-190°C ca. 13 min. backen.

Cocunut Macaroons

Level
1
Easy

Personen
6
Serves

Zubereitung
10 mins
Preparation

Inaktive Zeit
13 mins
Inactive Time

Ingredients:
4 oz. Margarine
4 oz. Sugar
2 tbsp Vanilla Sugar
1 tsp Pure Vanilla Extract
1 Egg
6 oz. Wheat Flour
3 oz. Starch
2 tsp Baking Powder
8 oz. Shredded Coconut
Some Lemon Zest

Preparation:
Mix all ingredients well until you get a firm and sticky batter. Use a teaspoon to form small coconut bowls and place them on a baking sheet with parchment paper. Bake in preheated oven at 350-375°F for about 13 minutes.

Quarkstollen

Zutaten:

500 g Mehl
250 g Magerquark
125 g Butter oder Margarine
125 g Zucker
2 Eier
125 g gemahlene Haselnüsse
1 P. Backpulver
1 P. Vanillezucker
eine Prise Salz
4 EL Rum
150 g Rosinen
je 50 g Orangeat & Zitronat

Zubereitung:

- Aus den Zutaten erstellt man zuerst einen "gehackten Teig". Dazu auf einem Backbrett das Mehl aufschütten und in dessen Mulde die restlichen Zutaten hinein geben. Mit einem großen Messer die Zutaten von außen nach innen mischen und mit der Klinge nach unten drücken.
- Aus dem gehackten Teig einen zusammenhängenden Teig formen und in zwei Hälften teilen.
- Ovale Stollen bilden und diese auf ein gefettetes Backblech legen.
- Im vorgeheizten Backofen bei 180 °C ca. 60 Min backen.
- Nach dem Erkalten dick mit Puderzucker bestreuen.

Curd Stolle

Level
1
Easy

Personen
6
Serves

Zubereitung
10 mins
Preparation

Inaktive Zeit
60 mins
Inactive Time

Ingredients:

18 oz.(4 1/4 cups) flour
9 oz. (1 1/8 cups) low-fat quark (or curd)
5 oz. (1/2 cup) butter or margarine
5 oz. (1 1/4 cups) sugar
2 eggs
5 oz. (1 cup) finely ground hazelnuts
1 package baking powder
1 TBSP vanilla sugar
a pinch of salt
4 TBSP rum
6 oz. (3/4 cups) of raisins
each 2 oz. of candied orange & lemon peel

Preparation:

- From these ingredient one first creates a "chopped dough". This is done by putting the flour onto a baking sheet the putting the rest of the ingredients into a depression in the flour. Use a large knife to mix the ingredients, from the outside to the inside, pressing it down with the blade.
- Form this chopped dough into a single piece of dough then divide it into two halves.
- Form oval stollen and put them on a greased baking sheet.
- Bake in a preheated oven at 350 °F for about 60 mins.
- Once the stollen have cooled off, put a thick coat of powered sugar on them.

Christmas

Glühwein

Zutaten:
1 l Rotwein
2-3 Zimtstangen
1 TL Gewürznelken
1 EL Sternanis
2-4 EL Zucker
2 Orangen
1 Zitrone

Zubereitung:
Rotwein mit den Gewürzen und dem Zucker in einen Topf geben, und langsam erwärmen. Den Deckel halb geschlossen oben auflegen. Die Flüssigkeit darf nicht kochen! Saft einer Orange auspressen und dazugeben. Die restliche Orange und Zitrone in Scheiben schneiden und mit erwärmen.Ca. 15-20 min. lang erwärmen, damit alle Aromen freigesetzt werden können.

German Mulled Wine

Level
1
Easy

Personen
6
Serves

Zubereitung
5 mins
Preparation

Inaktive Zeit
20 mins
Inactive Time

Ingredients:
1 qt Red Wine
2-3 Cinnamon Sticks
1 tsp Cloves
1 tbsp Aniseed
2-4 tbsp Sugar
2 Oranges
1 Lemon

Preparation:
In a pot heat red wine with spices. Make sure that it does not start cooking. Place a lid on pot, but do not close completely. Add orange juice of 1 Orange. Cut other Orange and Lemon to small lices and add to Wine Mix. Heat everything for about 15-20 mins. in order to give aromas to the "Glühwein".

Lebkuchen

Zutaten:
200 g Zucker
3 Eier
1 TL Vanilleextrakt
60 g zerlassene Butter
375 g Bienenhonig
1-2 Pkg. Lebkuchengewürz
100 g fein gemahlene Mandeln
etwas geriebene Zitronenschale
500 g Mehl
1/2 TL Backpulver
200 g kleine Schokostückchen (Bitterschokolade)
Vollmilch-Glasur

Zubereitung:
Eier, Zucker und Vanille schaumig rühren. Die Butter, Honig sowie Lebkuchengewürz unterrühren. Mandeln, Zitrone, gesiebtes Mehl und Backpulver mischen und der Eiermasse unterrühren. Zuletzt Schokostücken untermischen. Die Masse auf ein gefettetes Backblech aufstreichen. Im vorgeheizten Backofen bei 190°C ca. 30 min. backen. Nach dem Abkühlen mit der Schokoladenglasur bestreichen.

Lebkuchen

Level
1
Easy

Personen
12
Serves

Zubereitung
15 mins
Preparation

Inaktive Zeit
30 mins
Inactive Time

Ingredients:
8 oz. Sugar
3 Eggs
1 tsp Vanilla Extract
2 1/2 oz. Melted Butter
13 1/2 oz. Honey
1-2 Pkg. Lebkuchenspice (from a German Deli)
4 oz. Finely Ground Almonds
Some Lemon Peel
18 oz. Flour
1/2 tsp Baking Powder
8 oz. semi-sweet Chocolate Chips
Sweet Dipping Chocolate

Preparation:
Beat eggs, sugar and vanilla until fluffy. Mix in butter, honey, Lebkuchenspice. In a bowl mix almonds, lemmon peel, flour and baking powder and add to egg mixture. At last mix in chocolate chips. Fill batter in greased baking sheet. Bake in preheated oven at 375°F for about 30 mins. Let cool down. Cover with dipping chocolate.

New Year's Eve

Hefezöpfe

Zutaten:
500 g Mehl
30 g Hefe
60 g Zucker
250 ml Milch
60 g Butter
1 Ei
1 Prise Salz
Abgeriebene Schale einer Zitrone
1 Eigelb
Etwas Butter
(150 g Rosinen)

Zubereitung:
- In einer Teigschüssel das Mehl, Hefe, Zucker sowie lauwarme Milch, geschmolzene Butter, Salz und Zitronenschale, Ei (Zimmertemperatur) und ggf. Rosinen gut verkneten. Den Teig schlagen, bis er Blasen wirft.
- Danach zugedeckt an einem warmen Ort ca. 1 Stunde gehen lassen.
- Aus dem Teig jeweils 3 Stränge von gleicher Länge formen. Die Enden zusammendrücken und einen Zopf flechten.
- Den Zopf auf das gefettete Backblech legen und mit einem Tuch zugedeckt nochmals 30 min. gehen lassen.
- Den Backofen auf 220 °C vorheizen. Zuletzt mit dem Eigelb bestreichen. Ca. 30 Min goldbraun backen.

Level
1
Easy

Personen
4
Serves

Zubereitung
15 mins
Preparation

Inaktive Zeit
120 mins
Inactive Time

Ingredients:
500 g Flour
30 g Yeast
60 g Sugar
250 ml of Milk
60 g Butter
1 Egg
1 pinch of Salt
Grated peel of 1 Lemon
1 Egg Yolk
Some Butter
(6 oz. raisins)

Preparation:
- In a pastry bowl put in flour, yeast, sugar, lukewarm milk, melted butter, salt, lemon peel, egg and if desired raisins and knead to form a fluffy dough. Beat the dough until it develops bubbles.
- Cover the dough and allow it to rise in a warm location for about 1 hour.
- Form for each yeast plait three dough strands with the same length. Braid the strands together into a plait and press the ends together.
  Place the plait on a greased baking sheet.
- Cover with kitchen towel and let rise for about 30 mins.
- Preheat the oven to 425 °F. At last brush it with egg yolk. Bake for about 30 mins.

Menü-Vorschläge

Thema	Vorspeise	Hauptgang	Nachspeise
Topic	**Starters**	**Entrée**	**Dessert**

Vegetarisch
Vegetarian

p. 51   p. 65   p. 123

Apfel-Möhren Salat
Apple-Carrot Salad

Linsen & Spätzle
Sour Lentils & Spaetzle

Ofenschlupfer
Oven Dessert

Fleisch
Meat Lovers

p. 98   p. 86   p. 113

Gefüllte Pfannkuchen
Filled Meat-Pancakes

Gulasch mit Pilzen
Goulash with Mushrooms

Kauzen mit Speck
Kauzen with Bacon

Viel Aroma
Full Flavored

p. 45   p. 97   p. 147

Leberknödelsuppe
Liver Dumpling Soup

Sauerbraten
Sour Marinated Pot Roast

Johannisbeerkuchen
Current Cake

Menu Suggestions

Thema **Topic**	Vorspeise **Starters**	Hauptgang **Entrée**	Nachspeise **Dessert**	

Für Eilige
Express

p. 55   p. 94   p. 131

Feldsalat mit Erdbeeren
Nut Lettuce & Strawberries

Nürnberger Würste & Kraut
Nuremberg Sausages

Biskuitwaffeln
Biscuit Waffles

Feiertage
Holiday

p. 73   p. 88   p. 150

Maultaschen Suppe
Filled Pasta Squares in Broth

Rehbraten
Roast Venison

Bienenstich
Bee Sting Cake

Claudia's Auswahl
Claudia's Pick

p. 41   p. 83   p. 139

Suppe mit Kräuterflädle
Broth with Herbal Pancakes

Rindsrouladen
Beef Roulade

Apfelstrudel
Apple Strudel

Menü-Baukasten

Menu Kit

Beilagen
Sides

Menü-Baukasten

Hauptspeisen

Mains

Seite/Page
94

Seite/Page
105

Seite/Page
126

Seite/Page
97

Seite/Page
106

Seite/Page
128

Seite/Page
98

Seite/Page
121

Seite/Page
16

Seite/Page
101

Seite/Page
123

Seite/Page
16

Seite/Page
103

Seite/Page
124

Seite/Page
16

Hauptspeisen
Mains

Menü-Baukasten

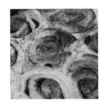

Cakes & Pastry
Kuchen & Gebäck

Seite/Page
143

Seite/Page
152

Seite/Page
169

Seite/Page
145

Seite/Page
155

Seite/Page
175

Seite/Page
147

Seite/Page
156

Seite/Page
179

Seite/Page
148

Seite/Page
159

Seite/Page
171

Seite/Page
151

Seite/Page
161

Seite/Page
163

Lexikon

German	English	German	English
Anis	aniseed	Kartoffel	potato
Apfel	apple	Kerbel	chervil
Bärlauch	ramsons; wild garlic	Kirsche	cherry
Banane	banana	Knoblauch	garlic
Basilikum	basil	Kohlrabi	kohlrabi
Birne	pear	Kopfsalat	boston lettuce
Blumenkohl	cauliflower	Koriander	cilantro
Bohnenkraut	savory	Kraut	cabbage
Brokkoli	broccoli	Kresse	cress; pepperweed
Brombeere	blackberry	Kümmel	caraway
Butter	butter	Kürbis	pumpkin
Dill	dill	Lauch	leek
Endivie	endive	Lavendel	lavender
Erbse	pea	Liebstöckel (Maggikraut)	lovage
Erdbeere	strawberry	Linse	lentil
Essig	vinegar	Loorbeerblatt	bay leaf
Essiggurke	pickle; gherkin	Majoran	marjoram
Feldsalat	mache; lamb´s lettuce	Mandeln	almond
Fenchel	fennel	Margarine	margarine
Frühlingszwiebel	scallion	Meerrettich	horse radish
Gekörnte Brühe	instant broth	Mehl	flour
Gurke	cucumber	Minze	mint
Haselnuss	hazelnut	Mirabelle	mirabelle plum
Heidelbeere	blueberry	Mohrrübe (Möhre)	carrot
Himbeere	raspberry	Muskatnuss	nutmeg
Holunder	elder	Nelke	clove
Honig	honey	Paprika	bell pepper; paprika
Ingwer	ginger	Petersilie	parsley
Joghurt	yogurt	Pfeffer	pepper
Johannisbeere	currant	Pflanzenöl	vegetable oil
Kakao	cocoa; cacao	Pflaume	plum
Kapern	capers	Porree	leeks

Preiselbeere	lingonberry; cranberry	Zitrone	lemon
Radieschen	radish	Zitronenmelisse	lemon balm
Rhabarber	rhubarb	Zucchini	zucchini; summer squash
Rosenkohl	raisin	Zucker	sugar
Rosine	Brussels sprout	Zwetschge	damson
Rosmarin	rosemary	Zwiebel	onion
Rote Bete	beet	*******************	*******************
Rotkohl	red cabbage	abgiessen; abtropfen	to drain
Rucola	arugula	abschöpfen	to ladle
Salat	salad	backen	to bake
Safran	saffron	braten (in der Pfanne)	to fry
Sahne	cream	entkernen	to core; pit; deseed
Salbei	sage	erhitzen	to heat
Salz	salt	frittieren	to deep-fry
Saure Sahne	sour cream	Hobel	mandoline slicer
Schalotte	shallot	in Scheiben schneiden	to slice
Schattenmorelle	morello cherry	in Würfel schneiden	to dice
Schnittlauch	chives	klein hacken	to chopp
Sellerie	celery	köcheln	to simmer
Senf	mustard	kochen	to cook
Spargel	asparagus	kurz anbraten	to sauté
Speck	bacon	mahlen	to ground
Spinat	spinach	Reibe	grater
Sternanis	star anise	reiben	to grate
Thymian	thyme	rösten	to roast
Tomate	tomato	Rührgerät	mixer
Traube	grape	Schaumkelle	skimmer
Vanille(schote)	vanilla bean/pod	schmoren	to simmer
Wacholderbeere	juniper berry	schneiden	to cut
Walnuss	walnut	Schöpflöffel	ladle
Wein	wine	Wellholz	rolling pin
Zimt	cinnamon	Zange	tongs

Verzeichnis A-Z

Index A-Z

17186981R00115

Printed in Poland
by Amazon Fulfillment
Poland Sp. z o.o., Wrocław